101 THINGS
YOU DIDN'T
KNOW ABOUT THE
CIVIL WAR

101 THINGS YOU DIDN'T KNOW ABOUT THE CIVIL WAR

Places, Battles, Generals—Essential Facts
about the War that Divided America

THOMAS TURNER, PH.D.

Adams Media
Avon, Massachusetts

Published by Adams Media, an F+W Publications Company
57 Littlefield Street, Avon, MA 02322
www.adamsmedia.com.

Contains material adopted and abridged from *The Everything® Civil War Book*, by Donald Vaughan,
Copyright © 2000, F+W Publications, Inc.

ISBN 10: 1-59869-320-4
ISBN 13: 978-1-59869-320-1

Printed in Canada.
J I H G F E D C B A

Library of Congress Cataloging-in-Publication Data
Turner, Thomas Reed
101 things you didn't know about the Civil War /
Thomas R. Turner.
p.   cm.
ISBN-13: 978-1-59869-320-1 (pbk.)
ISBN-10: 1-59869-320-4 (pbk.)
1. United States—History—Civil War, 1861–1865—Miscellanea.
I. Title. II. Title: One hundred and one things you didn't know
about the Civil War. III. Title: One hundred one things
you didn't know about the Civil War.
E468.9.T87 2007
973.7—dc22   2007002719

This publication is designed to provide accurate and authoritative information with regard to the subject matter covered. It is sold with the understanding that the publisher is not engaged in rendering legal, accounting, or other professional advice. If legal advice or other expert assistance is required, the services of a competent professional person should be sought.
—From a *Declaration of Principles* jointly adopted by a Committee of the
American Bar Association and a Committee of Publishers and Associations

Many of the designations used by manufacturers and sellers to distinguish their products are claimed as trademarks. Where those designations appear in this book and Adams Media was aware of a trademark claim, the designations have been printed with initial capital letters.

Interior photographs © American Spirit Images
This book is available at quantity discounts for bulk purchases.
For information, please call 1-800-289-0963.

CONTENTS

Introduction xi

PART ONE
The Coming of the War

1. It's Not Just About Slavery 2
2. Manifest Your Destiny 4
3. Insist, Resist 8
4. Voyage to Hell 10
5. The Confessions of Nat Turner 12
6. The Flack over the Fugitive Slave Act 14
7. Calhoun's Doctrine of Nullification 15
8. William Lloyd Garrison, the Liberator 17
9. John Brown's Soul Marches On 18
10. Frederick Douglass Follows the North Star 20
11. The Dred Scott Ruling. 22
12. The Many Voices of Abolition 24
13. Bleeding Kansas 27
14. Secession Surprises the North. 29
15. The Making of the Mason-Dixon Line 32
16. The Shrinking Union. 33
17. Elephant Stampede 34
18. The Underdog States 37
19. Teetering on the Line 38
20. Call to Arms. 39

21. Cabinet Players 42

22. Europe Chooses Sides 45

23. The Lincoln–Douglas Debates 48

24. Stephen Douglas, the Short Giant 50

25. Jefferson Davis, Leader by Default 52

26. Lincoln's First VP, Hannibal Hamlin 55

27. Davis's VP, Alexander Hamilton Stephens 57

28. Tough Times for Mary Todd 59

29. Belle of the Confederacy, Varina Howell Davis 62

30. Gods and Generals 64

31. The Fighting General Grant 66

32. (Un)Lucky Lee 70

33. A Company of Commanders 74

PART TWO
The Engagements of Wartime

34. A War of Amateurs 78

35. The Changing Face of Warfare 81

36. The Funding of the War 83

37. Fort Sumter Falls 85

38. Bull Run, Part 1 87

39. Shiloh, Bloody Shiloh 91

40. Antietam, the Single Bloodiest Day 94

41. Lee's Greatest Victory: Chancellorsville 96

42. Blood Bath at Gettysburg 99

43. The Rock of Chickamauga 101

44. Chattanooga, One More Nail in the Coffin. 104

45. Lee and Grant Meet in the Wilderness. 107

46. Countercharge at Spotsylvania 110

47. Atlanta Burns 112

48. The Battle of Nashville Closes the Western Front 115

49. Cat and Mouse in Petersburg 117

50. Warfare on the Water 120

51. Farragut Sails into New Orleans. 122

52. Naval Showdown in Memphis. 125

53. The Battle of Mobile Bay, "Damn the torpedoes, full speed ahead" . .127

54. The *Monitor* vs. the *Merrimack* 129

PART THREE
The Weapons of War

55. The Things They Carried 132

56. Muskets and Rifles 134

57. Handguns. 136

58. Swords and Sabers. 138

59. Artillery Fire. 140

60. The Ironclads 142

61. Non-Uniform Uniforms 144

62. Soldier's Clothes 146

63. Flags of the North and South 149

64. Music on the Battlefield 151

PART FOUR
The Horrors of War

65. Camp Life. 154
66. Chaos on the Battlefield 156
67. A Legendary Loss 157
68. Prisoner Exchange Rate 159
69. Andersonville Horror 161
70. Battlefield Medicine under Par. 163
71. Angels on the Battlefield: Clara Barton and Dorothea Dix 165
72. War Doctors: Little Training, Tough Job 167
73. African American Participation as Soldiers. 169
74. The Famous Massachusetts 54th Regiment 171
75. Ethnic Makeup of the Civil War 173
76. Chronicling the Civil War 175
77. Mathew Brady, the Father of Contemporary
    Photojournalism. 177
78. Espionage During the War. 179
79. Women and Children in the Line of Fire? 181

PART FIVE
The Homefront

80. Effects, for Every American 186
81. America on the Eve of Destruction 188
82. Changing Roles, Family Life 190

83. Ideological Rift Divides Families 193

84. City Life, Far from the Battlefield. 194

85. Surviving on the Farm 196

86. Lifestyle of the Landed Gentry, Plantation Life. 198

87. Slavery in the Bible? 200

PART SIX

The End of the Conflict, Reconstruction, and the War's Legacy

88. An End in Sight 204

89. The Final Battles. 207

90. The Hampton Roads Conference Calls for Peace 210

91. The Surrender of Robert E. Lee. 211

92. Lee's Final Order. 216

93. The Lingering War. 217

94. Arlington National Cemetery, a Final Resting Place 219

95. The Plot Against Lincoln 220

96. The Capture of Jefferson Davis. 222

97. The 13th, Abolishing, Amendment 225

98. Reconstructing the South. 227

99. The Freedman's Bureau Helps Former Slaves Adapt 229

100. Black Codes Slow True Sovereignty. 231

101. Johnson Takes Over: Rejoining the Union 232

Index. 235

Introduction

THE AMERICAN CIVIL WAR has often been called the "American Iliad" evoking parallels with the Trojan War. Just as that ancient contest became a defining moment for Greek history, the Civil War remains an epic moment in the American story. Some of the most revered names in our history emerged from the conflict: Grant, Sherman, Lee, Jackson, and Lincoln. Millions of Americans still visit the Gettysburg battlefield, Lincoln's Home in Springfield, Illinois, or the Lincoln Memorial. Almost a century and a half after its conclusion, the war's hold on the public imagination shows no signs of abating.

Perhaps part of the fascination comes from the fundamental changes that the war brought to society. While the conflict is partially the story of high-ranking statesmen and generals, almost no citizen remained untouched and not just the soldiers who fought and died. Women, for example, assumed new roles as their husbands went off to war and they were forced to run the farms and plantations or to work in factories. New and more destructive weapons were introduced including a Confederate submarine, the CSS *Hunley*, which sank the Union warship *Housatonic*.

Above all, however, the war allowed Americans to finally come to grips with the issue of slavery. Lincoln's immortal address at Gettysburg framed the purpose of the war with his references to the Declaration of Independence's avowal that "all men are created equal" and his hope that "government of the people, by the people, and for the people, shall not perish from the earth."

Nearly a century and a half later Americans still struggle to make Lincoln's dream a reality.

However, Americans should resist the temptation to dwell only on the glorious aspects of the Civil War. The deaths of 622,000 soldiers provide a stark reminder of the terrible price that the nation paid to keep the Union intact and to eradicate slavery.

PART ONE

THE COMING OF THE WAR

TO UNDERSTAND WHY THE CIVIL WAR OCCURRED, it is important to know what the United States was like in the mid-1800s. Unlike the 50 states we have today, the United States in the years preceding the Civil War was more like two separate countries living together as one. The North and the South were more disparate than they were alike, and these differences became increasingly vivid until, like a bickering married couple on the verge of divorce, they simply couldn't bear to live together anymore.

1.
IT'S NOT JUST
ABOUT SLAVERY

IT'S IMPOSSIBLE TO NARROW the cause of the Civil War to a single issue or act. Most people today, if asked, would probably say slavery. But while it's true that slavery was one of the most important contributing factors to the conflict, it was not the singular cause. In truth, the war was the result of myriad cultural and political issues that perniciously set the North and the South against each other for decades before the first shots of the war were fired.

A short 10 years before the war began, the vast majority of Americans in both the North and the South lived in rural areas rather than cities. Agriculture remained the biggest contributor to the nation's economy, and in this way, the two regions were very much alike. But between 1850 and 1860, the nation's burgeoning cities—particularly in the North—received a massive influx of immigrants. The number of farm dwellers increased by 25 percent during this period, while urban populations rose by a remarkable 75 percent. New York City, for example, reached a population of nearly 800,000 by 1860, making it the greatest city in the Western hemisphere.

As a result of this influx, the nation's population increased by 35 percent to nearly 31 million. But the South didn't benefit from this population spurt. By 1850, only a third of Americans lived in the South, compared to half at the beginning of the century. And of the nation's 10 largest cities, only New Orleans was located in the lower Southern region.

Indeed, the years before the war's onset saw some dramatic and fundamental changes in the nation's face. The North quickly took advantage of the amazing new products resulting from the industrial revolution, such as Cyrus McCormick's mechanical reaper, and great factories sprang up almost overnight as huge deposits of iron, coal, copper, and other important manufacturing basics were discovered and made available. It would be this industrial power, this ability to produce weapons and other goods, that would give the North a decided edge as the Civil War progressed.

The economy of the South, in comparison, remained based primarily on agriculture, with England and the Northern states being its biggest customers. (In 1852, a mere tenth of the goods manufactured in America came from Southern factories and mills.) Cotton, in particular, was a huge cash crop that brought large amounts of money to the region, though tobacco, rice, indigo, and other products were also widely grown. By 1860, the South was producing nearly three-fourths of the raw cotton used throughout the

On the Homefront **Many of these new city dwellers were country folk looking for a new way of life, but a greater number were immigrants from overseas, primarily Ireland and Germany, hoping to strike it rich in the Land of Opportunity.**

world—an estimated 1 billion pounds a year. But because the South lacked the manufacturing capability of the North, the region was forced to buy back the goods created from the products it grew, placing it at an economic disadvantage that angered many Southerners. This inequity played a large role in widening the division between the North and the South.

2.
MANIFEST YOUR DESTINY

AS THE UNITED STATES thrived and flourished during the early nineteenth century, the demand for expansion grew increasingly loud. The Western regions cried to be settled, and a growing number of Americans felt the nation's borders were ordained by God to extend from the Atlantic Ocean to the Pacific, a philosophy known as Manifest Destiny. If regions owned by other countries could be purchased, so be it. If not, they were more than likely to be taken by force. The Mexican War (1846–48), for example, was little more than a trumped-up conflict designed to wrest large tracks of Western territory from Mexico when that country refused to sell the desired lands. On February 2, 1848, the Treaty of Guadalupe

Hidalgo turned over to the United States 525,000 square miles of territory that would eventually become California, Nevada, Utah, most of Arizona and New Mexico, and parts of Colorado and Wyoming. It was the largest addition to the United States since the Louisiana Purchase in 1803.

The acquisition of this Western territory, as well as other tracts acquired earlier, created a growing rift between the North and the South in regard to the issue of slavery and, at the same time, states' rights. The South, naturally, wanted the new territories to allow slavery (years of planting land-depleting crops such as tobacco and cotton forced many Southern plantation owners to desperately seek new farmland), but the North did not.

The first solution was the 1820 Missouri Compromise, legislation that was specifically designed to keep both sides happy. The issue came to a head in 1819, when Missouri requested admittance to the United States as a slave state—an act that went against the Northwest Ordinance, since most of the territory lay north of the Ohio River. Worse, the addition of a new slave state would disrupt the balance previously enjoyed between the North and the South. Luckily, Maine asked to be admitted as a free state at almost the same time as Missouri, thus maintaining parity.

But it quickly became evident that the addition of new states would result in constant conflict. To settle the issue of Missouri's statehood and keep

Conflict of Interest   The Northwest Ordinance, enacted in 1787, stated that all territories north of the Ohio River were to be free and that those south were to be slave, and up to 1819, the two regions were equally divided, with 11 states each. However, pending growth required new action.

5

things peaceful for a while, members of Congress, led by noted orator and statesman Henry Clay of Kentucky, hammered out the Missouri Compromise, which admitted Missouri as a slave state and Maine as a free state.

However, the territory acquired as a result of the Mexican War would require another compromise 30 years later. The Compromise of 1850, brokered again by Henry Clay, with tremendous input from Daniel Webster of Massachusetts, did little to affect the institution of slavery in the United States, aside from officially prohibiting the slave trade in the District of Columbia. It admitted California into the union as a free state but allowed newly acquired territories to decide for themselves whether slavery should be permitted. Clay and Webster, who both opposed slavery but felt the issue shouldn't be allowed to tear the nation apart, struggled to make the Compromise acceptable to both the North and the South. However, neither side was particularly happy over the legislation. Some Southern politicians, such as John C. Calhoun of South Carolina, felt the Compromise didn't go far enough in securing the future of slavery, and they raised the specter of secession if things weren't eventually changed. The North, on the other hand, was appalled by a provision within the bill that required Northerners to return escaped slaves to their owners. But despite these objections, the Compromise was passed by the House and the Senate and, for a decade, averted civil war between the two regions, although tensions continued to rise.

The Missouri Compromise and the Compromise of 1850 both dealt in part with an issue of particular sensitivity to the South—states' rights. The federal government's right to decide important issues within a state was something with which many people, especially those in the South, vehemently disagreed, and the shifting balance of power between the federal government and individual states would remain a hot-button issue that would contribute strongly to the beginning of the Civil War.

The Tenth Amendment to the United States Constitution states that "the powers not delegated to the United States by the Constitution, nor prohibited by it to the States, are reserved to the states respectively, or to the people." To most citizens of the South, this amendment clearly prevented the federal government from interfering in a state's individual affairs—such as the institution of slavery. If changes were to be made, only the population of a given state could make them. The South felt the federal government was overstepping its bounds every time it attempted to abolish or otherwise deal with the issue of slavery in that region or in territories seeking statehood and balked loudly whenever challenges were made. In short, the proud Southern states didn't like being told what to do and begged simply to be left alone.

3.
INSIST, RESIST

WITHOUT QUESTION, THE ISSUE of slavery was one of the most volatile in the smoldering enmity between the North and the South. In the decade prior to the onset of hostilities, the voice of abolition grew steadily louder in the North, forcing the South into an increasingly stoic and uncompromising defensive position. The more the North insisted that slavery was morally wrong and should be abolished, the more the South resisted. But it would take the 1860 presidential election of Abraham Lincoln—and the South's perception that his administration was going to push for the abolition of slavery nationwide—to cause 11 Southern states to eventually secede.

Though the imprisonment of another human being for forced labor is unimaginable today, the institution of slavery has a long history in this country. Slaves were used for labor in the original 13 colonies (the first shipment of Africans were brought to this country in August 1619, arriving at Jamestown, Virginia, on a Dutch ship; they were possibly sold as indentured servants, though their plight was little different from that of outright slaves), and some of the United States' most revered figures, including George Washington and Thomas Jefferson, were slave owners. By the time of the Revolutionary War, slavery was legal in all 13 colonies, though those in the Northern regions were beginning to realize that the institution simply wasn't profitable. The five northern colonies eventually banned slavery outright, but it continued to flourish in the South, where slaves were used to work plantations and large farms.

Between 1510 and 1870, more than nine million Africans were captured and taken from their homeland for a life of slavery around the world. Nearly half of them were bought to the United States, primarily the Southern region, where the climate encouraged agriculture on a large scale. Outlawed in all Northern states by 1846, slavery quickly became the backbone of the Southern agricultural economy. The growing global demand for cotton, in particular, gave the institution new life at a time when many people in both the North and the South were starting to believe that it would disappear by itself if left alone.

Growing and harvesting cotton was hard, backbreaking labor, even with the use of Eli Whitney's cotton gin, and black slaves were commonly used to do the work that white farmers and plantation owners thought was beneath them. So important had cotton become as a cash crop that of the 2.5 million slaves engaged as agricultural workers in 1850, 75 percent worked at cotton production. So it's easy to see how the South, which had become so dependent on the labor force of slavery, was reluctant to give it up. By the time the first shots of the Civil War were fired, more than four million slaves lived in the South—approximately one-third of its population.

4.
VOYAGE
TO HELL

SLAVERY IS A MOST barbaric institution, and the import of slaves to the United States from west Africa was barbarism in its rawest form. Commonly known as the Triangle Trade, it involved exchanging rum, cotton, and other goods with Arab traders for West African slaves, selling the slaves to plantation owners in the West Indies, and returning to America with profits from the sale of goods, such as sugar and molasses, as well as slaves who had been "broken in" on the Caribbean islands.

The number of Africans who were snatched from their homeland as part of the Triangle Trade is impossible to determine, though the number of slaves brought to the United States is estimated at between 10 and 12 million. Many slaves were prisoners of war, others were criminals or debtors, and some were simply villagers sold by their money-hungry tribal kings and chieftains.

The voyage from Africa to the West Indies was the most harrowing and brutal portion of the trip. Slaves, having been first fattened up like cattle, were placed in a ship's hold almost like cordwood, with little room to sit up, much less stand. They were painfully shackled together, poorly fed (many

Sign of the Changing Times This seasoning process involved placing new slaves with old hands, who taught them what to do and made them more docile and subservient, a process that doubled their value.

slaves refused to eat the strange food they were given), given impure water to drink, and lacked any type of sanitary facilities. This lack of basic sanitation, combined with the vomiting that often resulted from fear and seasickness, created an almost overpowering stench in a slave ship's cargo hold and helped promote a wide range of diseases.

The voyage from Africa to the West Indies could take from 6 to 10 weeks, and many slaves died during the trip, their bodies simply tossed overboard to feed the sharks. If a ship's provisions ran low, the slaves were the last to be fed and the first to be discarded if necessary. Some slaves, when given the opportunity, threw themselves into the ocean rather than face a life of bondage in an unknown land.

The importation of slaves to the United States was banned by federal law in 1808, but the institution was able to continue right along as the slaves who were already here reproduced and kept the cycle going generation by generation, much to the delight of Southern plantation owners. The first United States census in 1790 counted 697,897 slaves. Twenty years later, despite a two-year ban on slave importation, the figure had grown by an astounding 70 percent.

5.
THE CONFESSIONS
OF NAT TURNER

IN THE ANNALS OF SLAVE REBELLION, the story of Nat Turner is one of the most dramatic in terms of intent, violence, and bloodshed. Raised by his African-born mother on a Virginia plantation owned by Samuel Turner, Nat Turner was taught to read by his owner's son. His father escaped when Turner was young and never returned, and Turner himself managed to escape at one point, only to return four weeks later of his own volition.

Turner became extremely religious over the years and began preaching the gospel to his fellow slaves, who came to call him the Prophet. In 1825, Turner reported having visions of the Second Coming of Christ, and other visions that encouraged him to kill his enemies with their own weapons. In 1831, a solar eclipse was interpreted as a sign from God that Turner should kill his oppressors and lead his people to freedom.

In August 1831, Turner and seven other slaves killed the entire Travis family (who had acquired Turner from Samuel Turner) with hatchets and axes, fulfilling God's "command" that he slay his enemies with their own tools. Turner and his followers then began terrorizing the area, picking up recruits from other area plantations until their numbers totaled more than 60. Their goal was the county seat of Jerusalem, Virginia, where they planned to take the armory, though they apparently hadn't thought past that.

Turner and his followers attacked area farms and plantations for two days, but the rebellion quickly became disorganized, with many members getting drunk on stolen liquor. Word of the rebellion spread through the area and Turner's followers were met by armed militia outside Jerusalem. Many were killed or captured in the ensuing battle. Turner and approximately 20 followers managed to escape the melee but were attacked again a short time later. Turner escaped again, this time with four followers, and hid in the woods for nearly six weeks before he was captured.

On November 11, 1831, Turner and 16 followers were executed by hanging for the bloody uprising, but their deaths wouldn't be the last. Slaves throughout the region were terrorized and attacked by federal troops, and more than 200 slaves were killed as payback and as a warning to others that any attempt at insurrection would be met with harsh punishment. Another bit of fallout resulting from Nat Turner's rebellion was legislation that prevented slaves from learning to read or write. An ignorant slave, the thinking went, was a docile slave.

6.
THE FLACK OVER THE FUGITIVE SLAVE ACT

THE FUGITIVE SLAVE ACT required federal marshals and deputies to aid in the capture and return of escaped slaves throughout the United States. It was included in the legislation as a way of appeasing the South, but it served only to inflame the angry passions in the North. Anti-slavery and anti-Southern sentiment skyrocketed in the Northern states as a result of the Fugitive Slave Act, and moderate abolitionists joined their more militant brothers in protesting what they saw as federally subsidized kidnapping.

These commissioners were paid on a case-by-case basis, $10 for each fugitive slave sent back to the South and $5 for each accused black person who was set free. As might be expected, this bizarre bounty system quickly became rife with corruption, and the number of convicted runaways far exceeded the number of blacks who were exonerated. In many cases, blacks

Sign of the Changing Times The Act provided for the appointment of commissioners to administer the cases of captured runaways.

were returned to the South based only on affidavits from Southern courts or the vague statements of white witnesses.

Abolitionists feared that the new law would lead to terrible abuses against Negroes living in the North, and they were right. There are reports of Southern bounty hunters arresting and sometimes kidnapping blacks who had lived in the north as free people for more than 20 years, or claiming children born in freedom to escaped slaves as "property" of their parents' original owners. As a result, efforts on the part of anti-slavery individuals to protect blacks living in the North increased dramatically, though many blacks, believing that there were virtually no laws to protect them, fled to Canada.

7.
CALHOUN'S
DOCTRINE OF
NULLIFICATION

IF ANY SINGLE INDIVIDUAL can be credited with instigating the Civil War, it is John Caldwell Calhoun, one of the South's most vocal states' rights and slavery advocates. Calhoun was born near Abbeville District in South Carolina in 1782. He received his education in the North, attending Yale University and receiving his law degree in Litchfield,

Connecticut. He entered politics at 26, serving two years as a member of the South Carolina legislature. In 1810, he was elected to U.S. House of Representatives as a War Democrat and received much publicity for his endorsement of United States participation in the War of 1812. Calhoun was appointed secretary of war by James Madison in 1817 and became vice president under John Quincy Adams in 1825. However, Calhoun's feelings toward the federal government began to change during his second term as vice president, this time under Andrew Jackson.

At issue was a protective tariff on imported goods that Calhoun felt exploited South Carolina. It was while fighting the tariff that Calhoun (who resigned the vice presidency to return to the Senate) developed his "doctrine of nullification," which held that state conventions could nullify any national law by declaring it unconstitutional. When Congress passed a second protective tariff in 1832, South Carolina embraced Calhoun's theory and nullified the new import tax. The resulting constitutional crisis included a threat by South Carolina to secede from the Union and counter threats from President Jackson to employ federal troops to prevent such an action. A compromise was proposed by Henry Clay, reducing the tariff but doing so gradually over a number of years. Congress passed the compromise, thereby deflating the crisis, but the conflict bolstered the issue of states' rights, which Calhoun saw as an effective way of protecting the South from Northern encroachment.

Calhoun remained an influential power in the Senate until 1850. His last speech—read by a colleague because Calhoun was too ill—argued against the Compromise of 1850, which Calhoun felt did not sufficiently protect the institution of slavery. Calhoun also noted that continued interference by the North on the issue would no doubt force the Southern states from the Union. Calhoun died from tuberculosis on May 31, 1850, just a few weeks after his final speech and a full decade before the civil war he had forewarned.

8.
WILLIAM LLOYD GARRISON, THE LIBERATOR

BORN IN 1805, GARRISON grew up in a poor but religious family in Newburyport, Massachusetts. He attended school until the age of 13, then became an apprentice at the *Newburyport Herald*. Within four years, he was writing hard-hitting essays for the paper's editorial page. In 1827, Garrison moved to Boston to write for a temperance newspaper called the *National Philanthropist*. There, he met abolitionist Benjamin Lundy, who brought him over to the cause. However, Garrison quickly broke with Lundy and his followers over the issue of slave colonization and started his own more radical branch of the abolitionist movement.

Conflict of Interest **Garrison believed in equal rights for all, not in shipping freed slaves back to Africa.**

Garrison is probably best known as the publisher of the leading abolitionist newspaper of its time, the Boston-based *Liberator*, which he began publishing in 1831. Though its circulation never exceeded 3,000, the newspaper was a leading voice in the New England abolitionist movement and carried wide influence. Garrison often described slavery as a criminal act and wrote that he did not want to act in moderation and that through the pages of his newspaper he would be heard.

9.
JOHN BROWN'S SOUL MARCHES ON

JOHN BROWN WAS A VOCIFEROUS opponent of slavery. Unfortunately, he was also more than willing to use violence and bloodshed to further the cause he so fervently believed in. As a result, Brown is best remembered today as the radical abolitionist who fomented a slave rebellion and tried to capture the armory at Harper's Ferry, Virginia.

Brown was born in Torrington, Connecticut, in 1800 to poor Calvinist parents. Though he received little schooling as a child, Brown would grow up to be a powerful and charismatic speaker who drew the attention of many prominent abolitionists, including Frederick Douglass.

Brown found his true calling as a radical abolitionist. In 1855, he joined five of his sons in the Kansas Territory to aid Free-Soilers in their fight against proslavery factions. His most notorious contribution to the battle was the 1856 slaughter of proslavery settler James Doyle; Doyle's two sons, William and Drury; Allen Wilkinson, a member of the proslavery territorial legislature; and Bill Sherman, another proslavery settler. Brown and his sons were never arrested for the killings, which came to be known as the Pottawatomie Massacre.

Brown later conceived a plan to lead a slave insurrection in the South and start a republic of free blacks in Virginia's Appalachian Mountains. The scheme was doomed from the beginning, but Brown was able to persuade a number of prominent abolitionists to back it. On October 16, 1859, he and 22 followers rode into Harper's Ferry. They planned to take the federal arsenal and armory there and use the weapons to arm slaves in a rebellion they hoped would spread throughout the South.

The group was able to take the poorly guarded arsenal and armory with relative ease, and Brown immediately sent two black followers into the countryside to recruit area slaves for his grand rebellion. But Brown's plans quickly turned to shambles. The thousands of slaves Brown had expected never showed up. Instead, the residents of Harper's Ferry surrounded the arsenal and armory, trapping Brown and his men inside. The angry mob then began firing on them, killing two of Brown's sons. By the following afternoon, Brown had barricaded what remained of his group, along with their hostages, in the fire engine house next to thee armory. A company of marines, led by Colonel Robert E. Lee, soon arrived to put down the insurrection.

On the morning of October 18, Lee sent in cavalry officer Jeb Stuart to demand Brown's surrender but Brown refused. Stuart then signaled for the marines to charge, and in the ensuing melee, two of the raiders were killed with bayonets. Within minutes the uprising was over and Brown and four remaining followers were captured.

Brown and his followers were charged with murder, treason, and inciting insurrection, and sentenced to death by hanging. Brown was executed on December 2, 1859.

10.
FREDERICK DOUGLASS FOLLOWS THE NORTH STAR

FEW PEOPLE FOUGHT HARDER for the rights of African Americans or were more active in the abolitionist movement than Frederick Douglass. A powerful speaker and writer, he edited and published the influential abolitionist newspaper *The North Star* for nearly 17 years and helped spread the word on the evils of slavery in numerous speeches throughout the North.

Douglass was born Frederick August Washington Bailey in 1817. His mother, Harriet Bailey, was a slave, his father an unknown white man. Sent to Baltimore at age eight to work as a house servant, Douglass was educated by the mistress of the house, who taught him to read and write. Escaping to the North, he made his way to New Bedford, Massachusetts, where he found work as a ship caulker and changed his last name to Douglass to avoid those who might try to return him to his owner.

At age 24, Douglass attended a meeting of the Massachusetts Anti-Slavery Society, where he spoke for the first time about his life as a slave and his escape. William Lloyd Garrison, the leader of the society, was taken with Douglass's speaking skills, and immediately hired him as a full-time abolitionist lecturer. Often Douglass would begin his speeches with these provocative words: "I appear this evening as a thief and a robber. I stole this head, these limbs, this body from my master and ran off with them."

After the war was over, Douglass continued to work for the cause of civil rights, clashing with President Andrew Johnson over his reconstruction policies, which Douglass felt didn't provide sufficient relief to long-suffering Southern blacks.

On the Homefront   **As the nation grew closer to civil war, Douglass strived to make slavery one of the key issues. And after war was declared, he worked hard to encourage blacks to join the Union Army, believing that participation in the war effort would go a long way toward abolition and full citizenship.**

President Ulysses S. Grant appointed Douglass to a number of government positions, including marshal of the District of Columbia and consul general to Haiti. Douglass died in his home in Cedar Hills, Washington, D.C., in 1895, at the age of 78.

11.
THE DRED SCOTT RULING

DRED SCOTT WAS A SLAVE who thought he should be free. His case went all the way to the Supreme Court, where the majority decision would keep him in bondage and further split the United States on the issue of slavery.

Scott was the property of John Emerson, an army doctor from Missouri. Emerson traveled frequently as part of his job, and between 1834 and 1838, he took Scott with him to army posts throughout the United States and the Western territories, including Illinois and the Minnesota Territory, where slavery had been outlawed by the Missouri Compromise. Scott returned to Missouri with Emerson in 1838 and after Emerson's death in 1843, he sued in the Missouri courts for his freedom and that of his family, with the argument that his stay in a free state and free territory had made him a free man. The Missouri courts ruled against Scott, but Scott's fight was just beginning.

Over the next several years, the case went through numerous lower courts, all but one ruling against Scott. The case was appealed to the Supreme Court in 1854, but due to a backlog of cases, it wasn't heard until 1856. Scott's position was argued by Montgomery Blair, who would later become postmaster general under Abraham Lincoln. The chief justice was 80-year-old Roger Taney, who had freed his own slaves in 1818 but still believed in the institution of slavery. Despite Blair's best efforts, the court ruled against Dred Scott, dashing his hopes for freedom.

When the *Dred Scott* ruling by the Supreme Court became public, Southern slave owners celebrated, confident that the issue had finally been laid to rest. In fact, so confident were many Southerners that slavery was now fully and officially endorsed by the United States government that bills to reopen the African slave trade were presented in Congress. In the North, people were stunned, disgusted, and outraged. Many saw the decision as a call to arms and began their abolitionist activities with renewed vigor; others who had tried to remain neutral on the subject of slavery found themselves compelled to join the anti-slavery cause. In that way, the *Dred Scott* decision actually helped bring about the end of slavery. It also helped Abraham Lincoln become the first Republican president by widening the divisions over slavery within the Democratic Party.

12.
THE MANY VOICES OF ABOLITION

THE CALL FOR THE END of slavery could be heard as far back as Colonial days, but the abolitionist movement didn't become a serious force in the North until the 1830s. Driven primarily by religious fundamentalism, early abolitionists felt that slavery was a moral abomination in the eyes of God and that the sooner it was abolished, the better. Not surprisingly, Southerners felt otherwise and viewed the growing abolitionist movement as just another Northern force trying to encroach on their lifestyle and economy.

The first official abolitionist organization, the American Anti-Slavery Society, was founded in December 1833 and included William Lloyd Garrison, the publisher of the abolitionist newspaper *The Liberator*, and industrialists Arthur and Lewis Tappan. The organization viewed early reforms of the institution, such as banning slavery from new states, as too limited and called for its complete eradication. Members also wanted full political rights for freed blacks. The abolitionist movement spread quickly, and soon there were more than 1,000 chapters of the American Anti-Slavery Society throughout the Northern states, boasting a membership of nearly a quarter of a million people. The word was spread through newspapers, lectures, pamphlets, and huge petition drives.

Some abolitionists, especially those in the most militant fringes of the movement, found that the society's philosophy didn't appeal to them.

Sometimes the violence went even further. In 1837, Reverend Elijah Lovejoy, the editor of an antislavery newspaper in Illinois, was killed by an angry proslavery mob enraged by his advocacy.

The Fugitive Slave Law of 1850 and the publication of Harriet Beecher Stowe's *Uncle Tom's Cabin* in 1852 gave the abolitionist movement renewed strength in the North as more and more whites came to realize the inherent evil, violence, and degradation of slavery. For a nation based on freedom, to hold an entire group of people in bondage went against the laws of both God and the Constitution, they cried, but again the South refused to listen.

A number of prominent blacks aided the abolitionist movement with tales of brutality against slaves and the risks slaves faced in trying to escape. Frederick Douglass, in particular, lent a strong, intelligent voice to the abolitionist cause and worked hard to spread the word of freedom. Other prominent abolitionists included the following:

- **Theodore Parker** was a Boston minister who encouraged his parishioners to help runaway slaves any way they could.

- **Sojourner Truth** (real name: Isabella Baumfree) was an illiterate slave who fled her New York owner in the 1820s and spent most of the rest of her life lecturing on the horrors of slavery.

- **Charles Calistus Burleigh** was an attorney who, at age 24, became a lecturer for the Middlesex Anti-Slavery Society in Massachusetts.

- **Harriet Tubman** was a small yet scrappy Maryland slave who ran away from her master in 1849 and spent the better part of her life helping other slaves reach freedom through the Underground Railroad.

Interestingly, the South had its share of abolitionist activity too. In the late 1820s, Southern abolitionist groups actually outnumbered Northern groups, with many important Southerners freeing their slaves and assisting colonization efforts. And in 1832, the Virginia legislature debated a proposal for gradual, compensatory emancipation that would have become effective in 1861. Obviously, the legislation didn't succeed, and the Southern abolitionist movement slowly died. Over the years, the South first adopted a defensive attitude toward slavery, then attempted to show that slavery, far from being evil, was actually good for the economy and for the slaves themselves. Of course, the more the South tried to defend slavery, the louder the cry for its destruction by Northern abolitionists.

On the Homefront   **Many abolitionists faced violent reaction in both the North and the South, and it wasn't uncommon for abolitionist-newspaper printing presses to be seized and newspaper offices to be ransacked.**

13.
BLEEDING
KANSAS

THE NORTH AND THE SOUTH managed an uneasy but peaceful coexistence on the issue of slavery for a long time, but as the nineteenth century progressed and the nation began to expand westward, slavery became an increasingly sensitive topic, with Northern abolitionists pushing harder and harder for slavery's elimination.

The issue reached the boiling point in 1854, when part of the land acquired in the Louisiana Purchase was divided into two territories, Kansas and Nebraska, along the 40th parallel. The Kansas-Nebraska Act, written by Illinois Senator Stephen Douglas, who some historians have claimed had a vested financial interest in opening up the territory because of railroad investments, all but voided the Missouri Compromise of 1820 and introduced the concept of popular sovereignty—the right of a people organizing as a state to decide by popular vote whether to allow slavery.

Kansas was the first to test the concept, voting overwhelmingly to become a free state. Proslavery advocates, however, refused to accept the popular vote and poured into the territory from nearby slave states such as Missouri in an attempt to shift the balance. In the North, these proslavery troublemakers were known as border ruffians, and they gave free-soil settlers no end of grief. Violence and bloodshed became common as proslavery and antislavery factions battled throughout the Kansas wilderness, earning the region the nickname "Bleeding Kansas." More than 200 people died in the vicious guerrilla warfare. In one of the most horrifying acts of mayhem, radical abolitionist John Brown, four of his sons, and two comrades shot and hacked to death with broadswords five proslavery settlers near Pottawatomie Creek on May 24, 1856, in retaliation for a raid by proslavery forces in the town of Lawrence.

It could be said that the fighting that occurred in the Kansas territory was the first of the Civil War because it strongly reflected the issues and sentiments that would eventually lead to Southern secession.

14.
SECESSION SURPRISES THE NORTH

THOUGH THE SOUTHERN STATES had threatened to secede from the Union over various issues (particularly slavery and states' rights) for many, many years, it caught the world by surprise when they actually did so. The straw that broke the Southern camel's back was the election of Abraham Lincoln, a Republican and avowed opponent of slavery who was supported by many vocal abolitionists. Fearful that the North, which was richer, more populous, and industrial, would even more insistently impose its will against them, the Southern states felt they had no recourse but to pull away from the Union and form their own nation. They had the right to do so, many felt, because sovereign states had formed the Union, and thus any state that felt oppressed by the federal government could justly withdraw rather than submit to laws it deemed harmful.

Of course, the federal government felt otherwise, deeming secession a treasonous act. But President James Buchanan (1791–1868), considered by most historians an average statesman at best, was loathe to do anything about it, preferring instead to run out the final days of his term as quietly as possible and then turn things over to the newly elected Lincoln. Buchanan did say that he felt the Southern states had no legal right to secede, but he also claimed that he lacked the authority to stop them and was less than anxious to start a war over the issue while he was still in the White House. One of his last acts as president was to call for a national referendum—a time-killer guaranteed to stave off the whole mess until Lincoln could take office—on whether force should be used to preserve the Union. Buchanan did refuse to turn over Fort Sumter, located in Charleston Harbor, to a rebellious South Carolina, though he managed to foul up even that endeavor by failing to reinforce the compound with men and supplies and leaving its commanding officer with less than clear orders on how to proceed.

It's interesting to note that as the presidential election of 1860 grew nearer, the warning bell of Southern secession rang louder and louder. Southern newspapers increasingly advocated withdrawal from the Union as it became clear that Lincoln was the front-runner, but most Northern leaders failed to heed these omens, having heard them so often in the past. Lincoln refused to issue any kind of statement that might appease the frightened South during his campaign, though his opponent, Stephen Douglas, took the threats seriously. When Republicans overwhelmingly won October state elections in Pennsylvania, Ohio, and Indiana, Douglas realized that Lincoln's presidential victory was a foregone conclusion, so he immediately traveled to the South in a desperate attempt to prevent the

On the Homefront The common belief was that the South was simply beating its chest and would fall back in line once the presidential election was over. Sadly, it was not to be.

destruction of the nation. The majority of Northerners, on the other hand, chose to view the bitter divisiveness through rose-tinted glasses.

South Carolina was the first state to secede, passing the Ordinance of Secession by unanimous vote during a state convention in Charleston on December 20, 1860. The convention drew a huge crowd and was attended by delegates from throughout the state as well as the governor of Florida, representatives of Mississippi and Alabama, and four former U.S. senators. The ordinance, which in essence lit the fuse that would ignite the Civil War, simply stated: "We, the people of the State of South Carolina, in Convention assembled, do declare and ordain that the union now subsisting between South Carolina and other States under the name 'The United States of America' is hereby dissolved." As the delegates left St. Andrew's Hall, Charleston literally burst forth in celebration. Crowds cheered, church bells rang out, and cannons were fired in jubilee. To most South Carolinians, it was the beginning of a new and wonderful era. Four years later, South Carolina would face the terrible wrath of William T. Sherman and his men, many of whom would take great joy in leveling large portions of the state they blamed for causing the Civil War.

Six other states quickly followed South Carolina's lead: Mississippi, on January 9, 1861; Florida, on January 10; Alabama, on January 11; Georgia, on January 19; Louisiana, on January 26; and Texas, on February 1. Following the fall of Fort Sumter on April 14, 1861, four more states left the Union to join the Confederacy: Virginia, on April 17; Arkansas, on May 6; North Carolina, on May 20; and Tennessee, on June 8. Together, these 11 states would make up the Confederate States of America.

President Abraham Lincoln wasn't eager to pit American against American in a civil war, but he also realized that eventually something would have to be done. The South would force his hand with the taking of Fort Sumter.

15.
THE MAKING OF
THE MASON-DIXON
LINE

THE MASON-DIXON LINE is named for Charles Mason and Jeremiah Dixon, the British surveyors who surveyed it between 1763 and 1767. Today, the boundary is generally regarded as the demarcation point between the Northern states and the Southern states of the Civil War.

The line, which runs along the northernmost border of Maryland along Pennsylvania and also includes the northern border of Delaware, was surveyed and established to settle a boundary fight between Maryland and Pennsylvania. However, the dispute lingered long after the Mason-Dixon line was created, with many Maryland residents insisting that certain lands in Pennsylvania still belonged to them.

Some historians speculate that the Mason-Dixon line inspired the South's nickname of "Dixie," though others believe the popular moniker was derived from the ten-dollar note issued by Louisiana, which was steeped in French culture and influence. As a result, the word ten was written as the French dix, and for a while, the ten-dollar notes were commonly known as "dixies."

16.
THE SHRINKING UNION

THE UNITED STATES OF AMERICA found itself a much smaller nation on June 8, 1861. That's the date that Tennessee—the last state to secede—broke Union ranks and joined its Southern sisters. On that date, the Union consisted of only 23 states and eight territories, including the Indian Territory between Texas and Kansas.

Even without the Southern states, the Union, led by President Abraham Lincoln, made up nearly three-fourths of the area known as the United States of America. Its chances of victory in the event of war were also considerable, at least on paper. According to the census of 1860, the population of the Northern states was nearly 22 million. Of that number, an estimated 4 million were men old enough to fight in combat if called. Even more impressive, the North had nearly 100,000 factories employing more than a million workers, and nearly 20,000 miles of railroad—more than the rest of the world combined—and 96 percent of the nation's railroad equipment. On the economic front, Union banks held 81 percent of the nation's bank deposits and nearly $56 million in gold. All of this strongly suggested that the South would be at a severe disadvantage should war break out. However, history would show that the South was more tenacious (and pugnacious) than originally believed and would frequently triumph against overwhelming odds. The North may have held the advantage in every conceivable way, but the Civil War was far from an easy triumph.

17.
ELEPHANT STAMPEDE

AMERICAN POLITICS HAS ALWAYS been an odd creature, with a wide variety of political parties and affiliations springing up throughout the nation's history. But the Civil War saw more than its share of political combat, particularly in the North.

Heated debate and partisan rancor over the Kansas-Nebraska Act of 1854 plunged Union politics into turmoil. Out of the carnage rose a new political organization known as the Republican Party, made up primarily of abolitionists, Whigs, Free-Soilers, and leaders of industry and banking. The party's key platform was a more central economic policy that benefited the North more than the South, but angering the South even more was the Republican Party's ambition to prevent slavery from spreading to the western territories. The Southern states immediately saw the party as a serious threat to everything they held dear, and their fear escalated with the election of Abraham Lincoln, the first Republican to hold the high office.

Sign of the Changing Times However, as with most things political, the Republican Party itself was torn asunder over the course of the war, dividing itself into three distinct splinters.

Conservative Republicans favored the gradual emancipation of slaves and kindness toward the South following the war. Moderate Republicans urged faster emancipation and some punitive economic and political sanctions. And radical Republicans sought immediate emancipation and harsh punishment against the South. Many radical Republicans saw the Civil War as a great opportunity to change everything they perceived as wrong with the South and hoped to make it more "Northern" during the coming Reconstruction by setting up Northern-run schools, hospitals, and even state and local governments. All three factions would test Lincoln's resolve as the war ran its course.

Like the Republican Party, the Democratic Party had also split into opposing factions—the Peace Democrats and the War Democrats. The Peace Democrats (also known as Copperheads, because they were believed to be deadly to the Union), considered the war unconstitutional and supported the Southern cause. Their position was that the Republican Party caused the Civil War by forcing the South to secede and did so only to strengthen its own power base and force racial equality, a phrase intended to frighten racists who might otherwise support the Union cause. Peace Democrats could be found in every Northern state, but the largest concentration was located in the Midwest, where fear of emancipation was strongest and anti-Republican sentiment ran deep.

On the other side were the War Democrats, who believed strongly in the Union cause and supported the Lincoln administration on most issues. Most War Democrats had no strong feelings regarding the institution of slavery in the South and felt no compunction about restoring the Union without emancipation if necessary. It's interesting to note that Lincoln delayed passage of the Emancipation Proclamation in an attempt to remain on friendly terms with the War Democrats and maintain unity in regard to the war effort.

Northern politics were fickle, and the ranks of the Peace Democrats and the War Democrats fluctuated wildly according to how the Union fared over the course of the war. During those periods when the North lost more battles than it won and public sentiment edged toward cutting Union losses and bargaining for peace, the number of Peace Democrats rose. But when the North began winning strategic victories and it appeared that the South was lost, the War Democrats became the party to join.

18.
THE UNDERDOG STATES

THE 11 CONFEDERATE STATES may have appeared small and weak in comparison to the far more industrial Union states, but what they lacked in size and population they more than made up with sheer guts and willpower. Together, the states had a total population of about 9 million people—a figure that included 4 million slaves, who certainly could not be expected to fight on the South's behalf should war break out. Because its economy was almost entirely based on agriculture—primarily cotton—the South had only 20,000 factories employing an estimated 100,000 workers. And, as noted earlier, the South's railroad system was inconsequential compared to the North's, with less than 9,000 miles of track—much of which would be destroyed during the war's waning days as a result of William T. Sherman's march through Georgia and into the Carolinas.

All of these factors would severely hamper the South's war efforts in almost every way. Its lack of industry, for example, would prevent it from manufacturing much needed war goods and its emphasis on cotton over food crops would help little in feeding its military personnel.

19.
TEETERING ON THE LINE

NOT ALL SLAVE-OWNING STATES immediately leaped on the secession bandwagon. Four border states in the upper portion of the region—Maryland, Kentucky, Missouri, and Delaware—were cautious in determining how to proceed after the first Southern states withdrew from the Union.

Even though slavery was legal in all four of the border states, the proportion of slaves and slave owners was less than half of that in the states that had already pulled away from the Union. Their sentiments on the issue weren't as strong as those in the Deep South, where slavery was much more an ingrained part of the lifestyle, and state leaders debated long and hard on which side to join in the coming conflict. Delaware was the first to act, quickly rejecting a Southern request to join the new Confederacy.

The Confederacy had a lot to gain by way of population, industry, and defense in getting the border states to join. Between them, the states would have added 45 percent to the white population (meaning more able-bodied soldiers), as well as more industrial output and military supplies. Their location, especially that of Kentucky and Maryland, would also have had tremendous strategic value should the Union Army invade. Maryland, in particular, was vitally important because it would have enclosed Washington, D.C., on three sides, putting a tremendous squeeze on the political power center of the North. But despite the pleas of Confederate leaders and more than a few battles, all four of the border states, though proslavery, eventually remained in the Union.

20.
CALL TO ARMS

TODAY'S ARMY IS CONSTANTLY at the ready. When orders to move out are given, forces leap into action with lightning speed. But things were considerably different at the onset of the Civil War. The North's army was fairly small, consisting of just 16,000 men, and the newborn Confederacy had no ready army at all. As the inevitability of war became clear, both sides set about bolstering their military might, forming armies made up primarily of volunteer state militia and selecting officers to lead them. It would prove a Herculean task.

Following the bombardment of Fort Sumter, Abraham Lincoln, believing the conflict would be over fairly quickly, called on the states to provide 75,000 militia at the government's service for a 90-day enlistment. The call brought a rush of eager young recruits anxious for a little excitement. It also forced the remaining Southern states—Virginia, North Carolina, Tennessee, and Arkansas—to leave the Union and join the Confederacy. Though their sympathies were with the South, all four states had hoped until the very last moment that the situation could be settled without the risk of bloodshed. That hope was dashed with Lincoln's call to arms.

The state militias that made up the Northern Army at the beginning of the conflict were an interesting but often motley group. Very few of them had received any type of combat training, and most of their drill instruction had been solely for show.

The typical militia regiment was made up of companies from neighboring towns, and many of the groups had never even met, much less trained together. This proved to be a serious hindrance, because warfare in the mid-1800s required soldiers to engage in highly intricate movements as they went from marching formation to fighting formation. Coordination was essential and could be instilled only through numerous and lengthy drills, something the majority of militiamen had never done. On the battlefield, they would prove to be next to useless.

Conflict of Interest   **The individual companies were often led by men with little or no military experience or background. Instead, they were chosen as leaders by popular vote or because they were of higher social status than the others.**

Field experience would quickly eliminate leaders who were unfit, but in the beginning, the armies of both the North and the South were composed primarily of amateurs leading amateurs.

Which is not to say that there weren't plenty of career soldiers on both sides, though the North had a difficult time deciding how best to use them. Lieutenant General Winfield Scott commanded the Union Army at the beginning of the war. Though battle experienced and an able strategist, he was now 75 years old and in poor health. After a few Union defeats and growing public dissatisfaction, Scott was retired and replaced by George B. McClellan. Lincoln would spend a lot of time shuffling his officers around.

The Confederacy was a little better off in terms of officer material because a great many of the Union's best military minds, most of them West Pointers, had defected to the South. As a result, Jefferson Davis, himself a West Point graduate with a lot of field experience, planned to use trained soldiers for his general officers as often as he could. One of his first appointees was Robert E. Lee, who had rejected command of the Union's principle army after Virginia seceded; Davis made him a full general in the Confederate Army. Other bold Confederate officers included Pierre Gustave Toutant Beauregard, appointed to command the chief Confederate Army in Virginia, General Albert Sidney Johnston, and General Joseph E. Johnston. Both Beauregard and Joseph E. Johnston would find their military skills hampered by a rancorous relationship with Jefferson Davis.

21.
CABINET PLAYERS

DURING THE EARLY DAYS of the Civil War, the Union and the Confederacy were governed by an intriguing collection of men. Following are some of the early cabinet members for both governments:

The Union

- **Secretary of State William Henry Seward.** As a senator from New York, he fought vigorously to prevent the spread of slavery in the territories but softened his stance somewhat in later years. Seward had hoped to be a presidential contender in the 1860 election but lost the Republican nomination to Abraham Lincoln. He was appointed secretary of state in a conciliatory gesture by Lincoln, a position Seward at first rejected. Once in, however, Seward worked hard to make his presence felt in every aspect of the administration. In 1861, Seward proposed a diversionary war with a foreign power, such as England or France, as a way of reuniting the nation; Lincoln quickly rejected the idea. Seward was attacked and seriously wounded on April 14,

1865, by an accomplice of John Wilkes Booth, but he recovered and was able to return to his job under Andrew Johnson. Seward died in 1872.

- **Secretary of the Treasury Salmon P. Chase.** One of the most radical and controversial members of Lincoln's cabinet, Chase served three years before conflict with Lincoln forced his resignation. Chase came to prominence in Ohio as an abolitionist lawyer who specialized in defending runaway slaves and entered the Senate in 1848. He later served two terms as governor of Ohio and became a prominent member of the newly formed Republican Party. Like Seward, Chase hoped to be the Republican candidate in the 1860 presidential election but accepted Lincoln's invitation to join his cabinet. Though he had little experience in finance, Chase was able to contain a mounting budget deficit and effectively finance the Union's war effort. He was also instrumental in restructuring the nation's banking system and helped push through the Legal Tender Act of 1862, which introduced a national paper currency that became known as "greenbacks." With his eye still on the presidency, Chase began a surreptitious move toward the 1864 Republican presidential nomination, but word leaked out, causing him tremendous embarrassment. He offered his resignation to Lincoln, who accepted a few months later. In December 1864, Lincoln nominated Chase as chief justice of the Supreme Court. Chase made one more failed bid for the presidency in 1868, then continued to serve on the Supreme Court until his death in 1873.

The Confederacy

- **Secretary of State Robert Toombs.** A rich and powerful Georgia plantation owner, Toombs resigned his United States Senate seat following the election of Abraham Lincoln and returned to his home state to assist its secession. Toombs hoped to be the first president of the Confederacy and was very disappointed when he was passed over in favor of Jefferson Davis. Davis offered Toombs the position of secretary of state, but Toombs quickly became bored (since the Confederacy had not been recognized by any foreign powers, there was little for the secretary of state to do) and remained in the position only five months before resigning to become commander of a Georgia brigade on the Virginia front—despite the fact that he had no military training. While secretary of state, Toombs urged restraint at Fort Sumter but became an advocate of all-out war once the first shots had been fired. Toombs narrowly escaped arrest at the end of the war by fleeing to Cuba and Europe, but he returned to Georgia in 1867.

- **Attorney General Judah P. Benjamin.** Benjamin was one of the most prominent and influential Jewish American statesmen of the nineteenth century. He was also a brilliant legal mind, attending Yale University at age 14. He became a successful attorney in New Orleans and owned a sizable plantation with several slaves. In 1852, Benjamin was elected to the U.S. Senate and remained in office until Louisiana seceded from the Union. He was appointed attorney general by Jefferson Davis, with whom Benjamin had been good friends, but the position didn't give him much to do, and Davis named him secretary of war in 1861. Benjamin was transferred to the State Department a year later and was influential in securing for the Confederacy some much-needed foreign loans. At the end of the war, Benjamin avoided arrest by fleeing to the Bahamas and then to England, where he settled and resumed his law practice.

22.
EUROPE CHOOSES SIDES

WHEN THE SOUTHERN STATES left the Union to form their own nation, it was hoped that the Confederacy would quickly be recognized as an independent republic by the major foreign powers—England, France, and Russia. Such recognition would add strength to its legal claim of independence, as well as provide much needed financial and weapons support for the war with the North. However, the issue was not an easy one to settle. England and France had defeated Russia in the Crimean War, giving them the greatest control over Central and Eastern Europe, and both would have been ecstatic at the fall of the United States government. Russia, on the other hand, needed the United States as an ally to help control its European enemies.

Sign of the Changing Times   **Shortly after the fall of Fort Sumter, England's Queen Victoria declared her nation neutral in the conflict but acknowledged the Confederacy as a belligerent nation, which meant it could buy arms from neutral nations and capture merchant and military vessels.**

The Union had expected from the beginning that England would disavow the Confederacy, specifically over the issue of slavery, which most Britons considered a loathsome institution. But while the British government acknowledged its disgust over the Confederacy's continued use of slaves, it ultimately decided on a position of neutrality primarily for financial reasons—British textile manufacturers were dependent on Southern cotton.

Much to the Union's anger, England's neutral position meant that it could still aid the Confederacy in a number of ways. One of the most damaging to the Union war effort was British production of Confederate blockade runners and warships, particularly in Liverpool, where Southern sympathies ran high. Technically speaking, the construction of these ships violated Britain's Foreign Enlistment Act, which forbade the construction and arming of warships in British territory for a belligerent power, but the South (and its British sympathizers) found a number of helpful loopholes.

One aspect of the Union's attack on the Confederacy was a naval blockade of Southern ports, designed to help strangle the South by preventing goods from coming in or going out. The blockade was only partially effective, considering the small number of ships in the Union Navy and the vast expanse of Southern shoreline, but it did strike an important blow against the Confederacy by preventing foreign businesses from legally doing trade with Southern states. As a result, a major goal of Confederate diplomacy in the first years of the war was to convince England to declare the blockade illegal so that the Royal Navy could come in and protect British trade with Southern merchants.

In 1861, the Confederacy hoped to force England's hand through an unofficial policy that became known as "cotton diplomacy." Knowing that England imported nearly three-fourths of its cotton from the South, Confederate farmers began withholding cotton supplies from British textile manufacturers. Their goal was to use economic extortion to compel England (and to a lesser degree, France) to recognize the new Confederate republic as an independent nation. It made sense in theory: No cotton meant no textile production, thus bringing the entire industry and thus the government to its knees. The concept dated back to 1858, when James Hammond of South Carolina made a speech suggesting that the withholding of cotton would cause England to topple "and carry the whole civilized world with her, save the South."

There was just one flaw with the plan: England and France both had more cotton than they knew what to do with. A bumper crop just prior to the war pushed prices down and allowed the two nations to stockpile almost two years' worth. In fact, as late as 1862, England was able to ship some of its cotton back to mills in New England. In addition, England had found ample new sources of cotton in Egypt and India, which had become part of the British Empire. British leaders contemplated the situation for a while and finally decided that the loss of Southern cotton was less of a problem than the loss of the more lucrative Northern industrial markets, especially during wartime. When all was said and done, "cotton diplomacy" netted the Confederacy almost nothing.

23.
THE LINCOLN-
DOUGLAS DEBATES

ABRAHAM LINCOLN WAS A GIFTED public speaker, but he found his talents put to the test in the now famous Lincoln-Douglas debates of 1858. Lincoln had been chosen by the Republican Party to run against Stephen Douglas for the U.S. Senate that year, and in an attempt to get his name out there and generate some much needed publicity, he quietly challenged Douglas—one of the most famous political figures of his time—to a series of seven debates on various issues, primarily the extension of slavery into the territories. Douglas accepted, but knew he was taking a big chance in doing so. The result was a confrontation between two well-spoken, outspoken men that is still remembered today as one of the most thrilling examples of American politics in action.

Conflict of Interest   **From the very beginning, they went at each other like verbal brawlers, often fighting dirty to make the other look silly or stupid. It was grand entertainment, and hundreds of people attended each debate simply to see what would happen.**

Slavery immediately became the hottest issue in the debates, and the verbal sparring often got extremely ugly by contemporary standards. Rather than fielding questions from journalists, as is the case today, the candidates themselves decided the tone and content of the debates.

Douglas immediately went on the offensive. He tried to discredit Lincoln on the issue of slavery by painting him as a rabid abolitionist who wished to put blacks on an equal basis with whites. He also suggested that Lincoln was advocating interracial marriage and hinted that if emancipation were to occur, the Illinois Territory would be overrun with freed blacks who would take jobs away from whites. Lincoln countered by calling Douglas's claims "counterfeit logic." He tried to explain his position as rationally as he could, noting that his call to halt the spread of slavery did not mean he was advocating any type of amalgamation of the races. He also reiterated his long-held belief that slavery was "a moral, social, and political evil" but that the federal government had no right to interfere in the rights of states in which slavery already existed.

Lincoln ultimately lost the Senate race to Douglas (who was elected by state legislators, not a popular vote as is the case today), but he ended up a bigger winner in the long run. His excellent showing in the debates and the fact that he provided Douglas with challenging competition made him a national figure and greatly increased his popularity within the Republican Party, which found his moderate stand on the issues a pleasant change from more radical Republicans like William Seward or Salmon Chase. Party officials would demonstrate their approval just two years later by selecting Lincoln as the Republican presidential candidate.

24.
STEPHEN DOUGLAS,
THE SHORT GIANT

STEPHEN ARNOLD DOUGLAS WAS short in stature but a giant among the politicians of his time. A gifted orator with a sharp mind, he unwittingly split the nation in half and pushed the two sides toward civil war with the Kansas-Nebraska Act which, as a senator from Illinois, he introduced to Congress in 1854.

Douglas was an influential senator who worked to help the North and South reach compromises on the most important issues of the 1850s. As chairman of the Senate committee on the territories, he found himself in the center of controversy over the issue of whether new states should be free or slaveholding. Douglas was moderate on the issue, focused more on expanding the nation to the Pacific coast and building a transcontinental railroad. To solve the deadlock over the issue, Douglas proposed the Kansas–Nebraska Act, which in effect repealed the Missouri Compromise and promoted the concept of "popular sovereignty," allowing the citizens of a territory to decide the slavery issue for themselves. The act was passed with less than successful results. Proslavery and antislavery advocates in Kansas debated the issue with guns and other weapons, bringing on a mini-civil war, which gave the territory the nickname "Bleeding Kansas." It was hardly the compromise Douglas had envisioned, and he accepted responsibility for the fiasco.

In 1858, Douglas ran for re-election to the Senate. He was opposed by Abraham Lincoln, who at the time was little known outside of Illinois. During the campaign, the two candidates engaged in a series of seven major debates over the issue of slavery. Douglas challenged Lincoln's stance on the issue while still promoting "popular sovereignty," which lost him much support among radical Southerners. Douglas won the race but at a heavy cost. His position on slavery alienated him from Southern Democrats and helped divide the party during the 1860 presidential election, in which Douglas again faced Lincoln. With his party split, Douglas didn't stand a chance and Lincoln won handily.

25.
JEFFERSON DAVIS, LEADER BY DEFAULT

JEFFERSON FINIS DAVIS FACED a long, arduous, and ultimately losing battle almost from the day he was selected provisional president of the infant Confederate States of America. The position called for a man of tremendous character, well accomplished in both governing politics and military strategy, and Davis was lacking in both areas. Davis did his best to establish the Confederacy as a self-sufficient, independent nation, but mercurial public opinion, infighting within his administration and military, his own personality quirks, and a war the South could not possibly win would prevent him from achieving his goals. He was a proud Southerner and states' rights advocate and, like most of his countrymen, bristled at the thought of any sort of Northern intrusion. During these years, a true Confederate was born.

Davis eventually became involved in politics and won a seat in the House of Representatives in 1845; he was supported and encouraged by his brother Joseph, a man of wealth and national influence. In that same year, Davis fell in love with and married Varina Howell, a pretty and personable daughter of a local gentry.

Davis was in office just a few months before resigning his seat to partici-pate in the Mexican War, where he saw just enough action on the battlefield to convince himself that he was an accomplished military man. Sadly, such was not the case, and Davis's own inflated self-image would spark numerous con-flicts with his more battle-seasoned military leaders during the Civil War.

Davis re-entered national politics as a senator from Mississippi and made a name for himself by strongly supporting Southern causes, including slavery (which he thought should be expanded into the territories) and states' rights. In 1853, President Franklin Pierce appointed Davis his secretary of war and during his three years in that office, Davis assumed an expansionist stance to foreign affairs, a position that reflected his opinion regarding the expansion of slavery. When his term was completed, Davis returned to the Senate, where he continued his vocal advocacy of slavery.

Despite Davis's unwavering support of Southern causes and his deep love of the South itself, he did not endorse secession and struggled through the Democratic conventions of 1860 to encourage some sort of compromise that would keep the Union whole. But with the election of Abraham Lincoln and the new president's statement that he would not tolerate the spread of slavery into any more territories, Davis knew that the line had been drawn. With a heavy heart, he resigned his Senate seat on January 21, 1861, and joined his fellow Southerners in seceding from the Union.

On the Homefront   **Davis had hoped to become commander of the Con-federate Army and was surprised when he was made provisional president— a position he assumed primarily because the bickering delegates could not agree on any other choice.**

Davis took the reins of the new republic with an eye toward total independence and international recognition, but he faced so many obstacles that his chances of success were next to nil.

His biggest problem was that he headed the central government of a new nation made up of states that wanted to retain as many rights for themselves as possible. In other words, the states recognized the need for a central government but didn't want to give it any power. Issues such as taxation, conscription of troops, currency, and the suspension of civil laws in the face of a war were a source of constant debate as the states tried to decide just how much authority their new government should have.

All of this, of course, made preparing for a war with the North all the more difficult for Davis, a man who lacked many of the basic leadership skills that made Abraham Lincoln the best man to lead the Union during this troubling period.

Worse, the South simply wasn't prepared for a long war. It had no standing army, lacked the manufacturing capability to produce sufficient arms and other necessary goods, and soon suffered from a Northern blockade of its most important ports.

The South fought valiantly, but the cause seemed all but lost by the winter of 1864–65. The Confederate Army was severely lacking in the most basic necessities, and the North had started several major assaults that threatened to bring the new republic to its knees. But even then, Jefferson Davis was confident that he could broker peace with the Union and save his beloved Confederacy. In February 1865, Davis bragged from the Confederate capital of Richmond, Virginia: "We may well believe that before another summer solstice falls upon us it will be the enemy who will be asking us for conferences." But just two months later, Richmond was on the brink of Union capture, forcing Davis and other Confederate leaders to flee.

26.
LINCOLN'S FIRST VP, HANNIBAL HAMLIN

HANNIBAL HAMLIN, ABRAHAM LINCOLN'S first vice president, would no doubt be a more prominent figure in American history had he not been replaced with Andrew Johnson during Lincoln's second term. Upon Lincoln's assassination, Johnson rather than Hamlin became the nation's 17th president.

A devout abolitionist, Hamlin was an influential lawyer and politician in Maine before being selected by the Republican Party as Lincoln's first vice president. In his home state, Hannibal held a number of important political positions, including state legislator, governor, U.S. congressman, and senator.

Unlike today, when presidential and vice presidential candidates stump together, Lincoln and Hamlin never even met until after the election. During the campaign, opponents angry over Hamlin's stance on slavery attempted to slur his name by suggesting that he was a mulatto trying to pass as white.

Hamlin and Lincoln got along well, though Hamlin was disappointed that the president didn't push for emancipation and the enlistment of black soldiers earlier in the war. Hamlin also anxiously awaited a more important role within the administration. Lincoln tried to assuage his feelings by seeking Hamlin's opinion on various issues but, for the most part, made the most important decisions himself. One important exception involved the Emancipation Proclamation. Lincoln showed Hamlin an early draft of the document and incorporated some changes in wording that Hamlin had suggested.

Eager for more meaningful work, Hamlin enlisted in the Maine Coast Guard while still holding the office of vice president. He hoped to remain on the ticket with Lincoln in 1864 but was removed by Republican officials as a matter of political expediency; the party sought the support of pro-administration Democrats and felt that the addition of Andrew Johnson, a Democrat, would keep them happy.

Hannibal Hamlin returned to the U.S. Senate in 1869, and he served in office for another 12 years before accepting an appointment as U.S. minister to Spain. Hamlin died in 1891.

27.
DAVIS'S VP, ALEXANDER HAMILTON STEPHENS

ALEXANDER HAMILTON STEPHENS of Georgia was an odd choice for vice president of the Confederate States of America. Though passionately proslavery and favoring states' rights, he was also a Unionist who didn't want to see secession destroy the country. In fact, following Abraham Lincoln's election in 1860, he called for a convention of all Southern states in hopes of preventing secession and attended Georgia's own convention in January 1861 to argue in favor of the Union. Ultimately, however, he signed the Ordinance of Secession.

Stephens was born in Georgia to poor parents and found himself an orphan by age 12. He was raised and educated by an uncle and showed great scholastic aptitude, graduating first in his class at the University of Georgia. Stephens studied law and passed the bar in 1834. Politics soon became a passion, and he was elected to the Georgia legislature in 1836. He served there for all but one year until 1843, working hard on behalf of his constituents. In 1843, Stephens was elected to the U.S. House of Representatives, where he made a name for himself with his unwavering support of slavery and states' rights.

Though he feared that secession would tear the country apart, Stephens had no choice but to follow his countrymen when Georgia split from the Union in January 1861. In February, he traveled to Montgomery, Alabama, and helped to draft the Confederacy's new constitution. His advocacy of issues important to the South, such as slavery, and generally moderate stand on most others made him appealing to the delegates of the provisional congress, and he was selected to be vice president under Jefferson Davis.

Stephens and Davis could not have been more different, and they did not get along personally or politically. In addition, as a long-time advocate of states' rights, Stephens could not abide Davis's attempt to create a controlling centralized government or his nationalistic approach to the war. He also disapproved of Davis's attempts to institute a draft, impose taxes, and suspend the writ of habeas corpus. As a result of these differences, Stephens spent very little time in the Confederate capital of Richmond, preferring instead his home state of Georgia.

During his tenure, Stephens tried to provide a strong national voice and advocated a number of sound political policies, such as the quick sale of cotton to Europe before the Union blockade of Southern ports went into effect. He also pushed for peace between the warring regions and led the Southern delegation at the failed Hampton Roads Conference in February 1865. During that meeting with Abraham Lincoln and Secretary of State Seward, Ste-

Sign of the Changing Times   **At the war's end, Stephens was arrested and imprisoned at Fort Warren in Boston until October 1865. After being freed, he returned to Georgia and was again elected to the U.S. Senate in 1866.**

phens urged the North and the South to end their differences and unite to fight the French in Mexico. His pleas were ignored.

However, he was refused his seat by radical Republicans in Congress seeking to punish the seceded states. In 1871, Stephens bought a newspaper in Atlanta and used it to attack what he saw as unfair Reconstructionist policies. Two years later, he was elected to the House of Representatives, where he served until 1882. Stephens was then elected governor of Georgia, but he died in 1883, just a few months into his term. In addition to his political successes, Alexander Hamilton Stephens wrote a very successful book on the Civil War entitled *A Constitutional View of the Late War Between the States*.

28.
TOUGH TIMES
FOR MARY TODD

MARY TODD LINCOLN WAS born in 1818 into a life of privilege. Her father was a wealthy banker in Lexington, Kentucky, and Mary grew up well educated and socially ambitious. At the age of 21, she moved to Springfield, Illinois, to live with her married sister. Her sister's father-in-law, Ninian Edwards, was the governor of Illinois, and Mary quickly became one of the most popular girls in their social and political set, which included a number of influential politicians.

It was in Springfield that Mary met Abraham Lincoln, by then a prominent lawyer with strong political ambitions and the drive to make them a reality. Mary realized Lincoln had great potential as a husband and politician. Their first attempt to wed was called off at the last minute, when Lincoln got cold feet. They tried again—successfully—on November 4, 1842. Lincoln was 33, Mary just 23.

Mary gave birth to Robert, the first of their four sons, just nine months after she and Lincoln were wed. Sadly, Robert would be the only child to survive into adulthood. Their second son, Edward Baker, was born in 1846, but he died four years later. The Lincolns would lose another child, 11-year-old William, in 1862 to fever and a third, Tad, in 1871 to tuberculosis. The death of William was a devastating blow to the Lincolns, and Mary, already delicate and overwrought, suffered a nervous breakdown that kept her bedbound for nearly 3 months. She eventually recovered but refused to enter William's room again. She began consulting spiritualists and seers in an attempt to con-

On the Homefront **When Lincoln was elected president, Mary did her best to fit in, but her snooty manner and taste for extravagance only alienated her from the general public. Mary was also prone to outbursts of temper and jealousy that greatly embarrassed her husband and his staff. One of the victims of her temper was the wife of General Ulysses S. Grant; Grant's wife couldn't stand to be in the same room with Mary.**

tact William in the spirit world and later told her half sister Emilie that the ghosts of both Edward and William visited her in the White House.

The war placed Mary in great conflict. As the wife of the president of the United States, she was an avowed and dedicated Unionist. But four of her brothers and three of her brothers-in-law served in the Confederate Army, resulting in a great deal of criticism that Mary found difficult to take. Still she persevered, attempting to maintain some degree of social life during the war's grimmest months—another issue that resulted in public criticism. No matter what Mary did, it seemed that there were always those ready to take her to task for it.

Her husband's assassination was one of the greatest emotional blows suffered by Mary Todd Lincoln. She was devastated by the incident, so overcome by grief that she was unable to accompany his body to Springfield, Illinois, for burial. Mary was left a wealthy woman after Lincoln's death, but she spent a great deal on frivolous things and found herself almost penniless after a few years. Congress took pity on her and granted her a liberal pension, which allowed her to live well, if not exactly in the wealthy manner to which she had become accustomed.

Following Tad's death, Mary plunged into such a state of depression that her eldest son, Robert, had her institutionalized for several months. Mary traveled some after that, then spent her remaining years with her sister in Springfield, in the same house in which she had met her husband some four decades before. Mary Todd Lincoln died on July 16, 1882.

29.
BELLE OF THE CONFEDERACY, VARINA HOWELL DAVIS

VARINA HOWELL DAVIS WAS a source of tremendous support for her husband, Confederate President Jefferson Davis, and for the Southern cause during the Civil War. It was a very difficult task, but she performed it with wit, humor, and grace.

Varina Howell was born in Mississippi in 1826. Her father was a wealthy plantation owner with Northern roots—her grandfather was an eight-term governor of New Jersey—and Varina grew up in a life of privilege and education. A bright and vivacious girl, she spent two years at a girls' finishing school in Philadelphia. At age 17, she was introduced to Jefferson Davis, a widower twice her age. They married in 1845, and Varina enjoyed the social whirl that came with being the spouse of a rising star within the Democratic Party. When the couple moved to Washington D.C., Varina fit in quite well and received some renown as a charming and witty hostess with a penchant for throwing spectacular parties. With her husband pre-occupied with politics, she also oversaw the affairs of their plantation in Mississippi.

After her husband was elected president of the Confederate States of America, Varina packed up and moved with their family to join Davis in Richmond, Virginia. Her role as First Lady of the new republic was considerably more difficult than anything she had previously experienced, but she proved adept at juggling her many responsibilities, most notably sustaining her husband during the course of the Civil War, a cause both knew was desperate from the start.

Like Mary Todd Lincoln, Varina Davis faced an onslaught of criticism from the press and the public. Because her background was from the North, there were those who felt that Varina didn't fully support the Confederacy—a false allegation. She was alternately accused of entertaining too lavishly during wartime and not doing enough to lift the spirits of her countrymen. Varina also faced challenges in her personal life. In 1864, her five-year-old son, Joe, fell to his death from the rear balcony of the presidential mansion in Richmond.

Varina was with her husband when he was captured by federal troops near Irwinville, Georgia, in May 1865. She spent the next two years fighting for his release from prison and even met with President Andrew Johnson, who was sympathetic to her plight. When Davis was finally released, he and Varina settled at an estate near Biloxi, Mississippi; the estate, named "Beauvoir," was given to them by a benefactor. Upon Davis's death in 1889, Varina turned the estate into a home for Confederate veterans and went to live with her daughter in New York City.

Varina Howell Davis published her memoirs in 1890 and continued to write for various magazines and newspapers. She died in 1906 and was buried in Richmond, next to her husband, who was well remembered by the people of the South.

30.
GODS AND GENERALS

IN TODAY'S U.S. ARMY, rank is determined by experience and expertise. But things were a little different during the Civil War. It was an era in which political favors were often repaid with military appointments. Many of the Union's early military officers were loyal Republicans, influential War Democrats, or everyday people demanding payback for some favor granted earlier. As might be expected, the majority of officers so appointed had no right leading men into battle, and during their relatively brief command, they only served to embarrass themselves and their respective war departments. The First Battle of Bull Run resulted in a humiliating Union rout when inexperienced officers panicked and ran in the face of the enemy, abandoning their men.

General Benjamin Franklin Butler is a prime example of wartime incompetence. A prominent Boston attorney and influential Democrat,

Butler used his influence to grab a military appointment. He managed some early successes but embarrassed himself mightily when, as military governor of New Orleans, he ordered the confiscation of Confederate property and was accused of stealing silverware from area homes and churches. Butler also succeeded in angering the entire population of New Orleans with his controversial "Woman Order," which stated that any woman who insulted or berated a Union soldier would be treated like a common prostitute. Butler was recalled by his superiors in Washington in December 1862 after corruption and bribery by Northern speculators became commonplace in the city under his administration. Butler was later given a field command in Virginia, and his embarrassments continued to mount throughout the rest of the war.

Not surprisingly, the incompetence demonstrated by many appointed officers did little to instill pride or confidence in the men who served under them, and morale in such units was often very low.

Several hundred officers were let go or resigned in the following months, making room for leaders with more experience. The practice of appointing officers, or electing them from the ranks (a common practice in volunteer units), continued, but at least the review boards helped establish minimum standards of competence.

Sign of the Changing Times   **The day after the Union defeat at the First Battle of Bull Run, Congress authorized the formation of military review boards to evaluate officers and remove those found to be unfit for command.**

The bad apples aside, many officers in both the Union and the Confederate armies proved to be outstanding leaders and military strategists. They led their men from the front rather than the rear, defined bravery in the face of overwhelming odds, and did all they could to advance their side to victory.

31.
THE FIGHTING
GENERAL GRANT

ULYSSES SIMPSON GRANT CAME out of the Civil War the savior of the Union and a true hero. So popular was he at the war's end that he was elected president in 1868, an astonishing achievement for a man who, prior to the war, failed at almost everything he attempted.

Grant was born Hiram Ulysses Grant in Georgetown, Ohio, in 1822. His father was a hardworking tanner and his mother a devoutly religious woman. Preferring horses to studying, Grant proved a skilled rider but did poorly in school. However, despite his poor grades, Grant managed to make it into West Point thanks to a recommendation from his local congressman, who mistakenly referred to him as Ulysses Simpson Grant in his letter to the academy. Grant liked the name and kept it.

Grant continued his tradition of mediocre grades while at West Point, graduating 21st in a class of 39, and was commissioned brevet second lieutenant. He was assigned to the infantry and sent to Jefferson Barracks, near St. Louis, Missouri, where he learned how to be a soldier. It was there that he met Julia Dent, who would soon become his wife. A year later, he was sent to the Southwest frontier, where he served until the beginning of the Mexican War. During that conflict, he served under Zachary Taylor and Winfield Scott. Both men taught Grant much about military strategy and combat, lessons that would serve him well later in life.

Following the Mexican War, Grant was assigned to a variety of distant posts, a situation that did little to instill in him a passion for the military as a career. He started drinking heavily while stationed at a post on the Pacific coast and resigned from the army after being reprimanded by his commanding officer.

Grant moved with his family back to St. Louis, where he tried a number of occupations with little success. Finally, his two brothers hired him as a clerk at their leather store, and there he stayed until the beginning of the Civil War. When the first shots were fired on Fort Sumter, Grant eagerly volunteered for the Union army but had great difficulty getting someone to assign him to a true command. Finally, in June 1861, he was made colonel of a regiment of volunteers from Illinois. Three months later, Grant was promoted to brigadier general and assigned to a command in Illinois.

The first military action Grant saw in the war was an attack on a Confederate camp at Belmont, Kentucky. However, the attack almost turned into a disaster when the enemy started to regroup as Grant's men broke ranks to ransack the camp. Luckily, Grant was able to pull them together in time. In February 1862, Grant led a very successful campaign against Fort Henry and Fort Donelson in Tennessee. During the latter attack, he uttered his now-famous proclamation, "No terms except an unconditional and immediate surrender can be accepted." From then on, the "U.S." in his name came to stand for Unconditional Surrender.

Thanks to his successful campaign against Forts Henry and Donelson, Grant was promoted to major general by President Lincoln. He fought in the Shiloh campaign, but his success there was almost accidental; it was superior Union numbers more than anything else that defeated more skilled Confederate troops. Union casualties were heavy during the battle, and Grant received more than his share of criticism. But Lincoln stood by him, noting, "I can't spare this man—he fights."

The Shiloh campaign tarnished Grant's reputation, but he was able to redeem himself and prove his skill as a military strategist with his amazing capture of Vicksburg in July 1863. This much-needed victory opened the Mississippi River to the Union and split the Confederacy in half. Four months later, Grant won additional victories at Missionary Ridge and Lookout Mountain in Tennessee. Congress was so grateful for Grant's successes that he received a gold medal and was promoted to lieutenant general. More importantly, Lincoln made Grant general-in-chief of the armies of the United States.

Finally in charge, Grant developed a plan to attack the Confederate army on three fronts: Meade and the Army of the Potomac would face Lee, Butler would lead the Army of the James against Lee's support, and Sherman would lead the Army of the Tennessee against Joe Johnston and finally into Atlanta. Rather than stay in Washington, where he felt out of place, Grant chose to lead by example and went into combat with the Army of the Potomac.

The Confederacy did not roll over under Grant's three-pronged assault. Both sides fought valiantly, and many battles resulted in extremely heavy Union casualties. But the officers under Grant's command did their jobs well, and the strategy eventually proved effective. Sherman managed to cut a wide swath through the South, severing Confederate supply lines and destroying anything that could be used to sustain the Confederate war machine. By April, the Confederate army was in desperate straits, with many of its soldiers literally starving. On April 9, 1865, Grant accepted Robert E. Lee's surrender at Appomattox Court House, effectively ending the war.

With the war's end, Grant was a national hero. He assisted in the Reconstruction effort, leaning toward a more moderate stance and chafing at many of the overly punitive policies instituted by Congress. In 1868, he ran for president as a Republican and won the election with little difficulty. However, Grant was always more of a military man than a politician, and his two terms in office were marred by scandal and accusations of corruption within his administration, though Grant himself came out relatively unscathed.

Sadly, Grant's final years were less than successful. He failed at a number of ventures and found himself so poor that he was forced to sell his treasured war mementos and write his memoir to put food on the table. His autobiography, *Personal Memoirs*, was a huge success, but Grant died from throat cancer in 1885 before he could enjoy any financial reward.

32.
(UN)LUCKY LEE

ROBERT EDWARD LEE STANDS out as one of the most conflicted commanding officers of the Civil War. A dedicated Southerner who turned down command of the Union army to remain faithful to his home state of Virginia, he emerged from the war a hero to the South despite numerous losses and near escapes on the battlefield. Though a fine leader and military tactician, a great deal of Lee's success during the war must be attributed to luck. Nonetheless, Lee managed to rally his army in the face of overwhelming odds and continued to fight valiantly long after the cause was lost. His remarkable dedication to the war effort typifies everything that made the South such a formidable foe during the four-year conflict.

Born in Virginia in 1807, Lee descended from a family that had more than its share of influential statesmen and soldiers. His father, "Lighthorse Harry" Lee, was a former governor of Virginia and a cavalry officer during the Revolutionary War. However, Harry Lee's death, when Robert was only 11, left the family somewhat impoverished, and Robert was raised by his mother, Anne, to whom he was extremely close.

A good student, Lee entered West Point in 1825, his admittance all but guaranteed by a testimonial letter signed by five senators and three representatives. Lee studied hard and graduated second in his class (and without a single demerit) in 1829. Because of his high grades, he was assigned to the corps of engineers (less talented students were usually assigned to the infantry) and traveled to a number of different posts over the next 17 years. During this time, he married Mary Ann Randolph Custis and started a family.

During the Mexican War, Lee was commended for his commitment to the various combat assignments to which he was appointed, and in 1848, he was placed in charge of the construction of Fort Carroll in Baltimore Harbor. Four years later, he was made superintendent of West Point. It was a highly coveted assignment, but Lee found the work unexciting and was transferred to the 2nd Cavalry Division in 1855, spending much of his time in Texas.

His superiors in Washington tried desperately to keep him as the Southern states began to secede and even offered Lee the command of the Union army, but he refused and resigned his commission. By June 1861, Lee was appointed a general in the Confederate army and advisor to Confederate President Jefferson Davis.

He stopped a Union advance from western Virginia and organized defenses along the coasts of Georgia and South Carolina. On May 31, 1861,

Conflict of Interest As the Civil War began to heat up, Lee realized that although he wasn't an advocate of either slavery or states' rights, he had to follow his heart and remain faithful to his home state of Virginia.

Lee took command of the Confederate army after General Joseph Johnston was wounded in the Battle of Seven Pines. He renamed it the Army of Northern Virginia and set about preventing Union forces from taking Richmond. It appeared to be a no-win situation, since Union General George McClellan had more than 100,000 men at his command, Major General Nathaniel Banks was moving on several important Confederate supply forces in the Shenandoah Valley, and Major General Irvin McDowell was camped just a stone's throw away in northern Virginia. In all cases, the Union forces far outnumbered the Confederate forces.

Lee's strategy was simple: He would combine his entire army against one of the opposing threats, defeat it, and thus disrupt the remaining Union forces. With more than a little luck on his side, Lee managed to push back McClellan's army. He then turned north to attack the Union army in the Second Battle of Bull Run. Both times, Lee was ably assisted by Thomas "Stonewall" Jackson, who so admired Lee that he once noted, "I would follow him onto the battlefield blindfolded."

The morale of his soldiers was remarkably high as a result of these victories, so Lee decided to continue his offensive with a northern invasion. Jackson captured Harpers Ferry, Virginia, but Lee's plans accidentally fell into McClellan's hands, forcing him to take a defensive position at Antietam Creek, Maryland. The ensuing battle was the bloodiest single-day fight in the war, and both sides took heavy losses. Lee was forced to retreat back to Virginia, where he was harshly criticized by the press.

However, things went better for Lee three months later, when he defeated Union forces at the Battle of Fredericksburg in Virginia. Troops led by Ambrose Burnside took longer than anticipated to attack, allowing Lee to secure important defensive positions in the nearby hills. The result was a devastating blow to the Union. Lee again saw victory against overwhelming forces in the Battle of Chancellorsville in May 1863, but success came with a heavy price: the death of corps commander Stonewall Jackson.

Lee was on a roll, and in June he attempted another invasion into the North. He succeeded in capturing the entire Cumberland Valley and other parts of Pennsylvania. But Lee's luck ran out in the Battle of Gettysburg, where he suffered a huge number of casualties in three days of heavy fighting and was forced to retreat.

In the spring of 1864, Lee faced Grant for the first time, in what became known as the Wilderness campaign. Lee was overpowered 120,000 men to just 60,000, and his troops were crushed by Grant's better-equipped soldiers in several battles. Despite his best efforts, Lee was forced to retreat to Petersburg, where he tried desperately to protect the Confederate capital of Richmond from Grant's ceaseless onslaught. His forces dwindled on an almost daily basis, but still Lee fought on.

In February 1865, Lee was placed in charge of all of the Confederate armies. It was a no-win situation, and everyone knew it. In hindsight, Jefferson Davis probably should have surrendered and tried to broker a peace treaty, but he felt confident that Lee could rally the troops and push on. For three hard months Lee did his best to protect Richmond, but Grant's overwhelming numbers and Lee's inability to get needed supplies finally took their toll. His men starving, Lee surrendered to Grant on April 9, 1865.

After the war, Lee was paroled home and indicted for treason. However, he was never brought to trial and was finally pardoned. He spent his remaining years as president of Washington College (later named Washington and Lee College) in Lexington, Virginia. There, among other accomplishments, he established the nation's first journalism and business schools. Robert E. Lee died on October 12, 1870, and was buried in the chapel he built on the university campus.

33.
A COMPANY OF
COMMANDERS

THE ARMIES OF THE UNION and the Confederacy were commanded by a large number of men. Following is a short list of other military figures of note.

The Union

- **George G. Meade (1815–77)** saw action at Mechanicsville, Gaines's Mills, and White Oak Swamp, where he was badly wounded. He returned to lead his brigade in the Second Battle of Bull Run and the

Battle of Antietam. Meade replaced Joseph Hooker as commander of the Army of the Potomac on June 28, 1863—just in time to lead it during the Battle of Gettysburg.

- **Joseph Hooker (1814–79)** was known by the nickname "Fighting Joe Hooker," which he greatly disliked. He led the Union attack at Antietam and was wounded; he recovered to command a corps in the Battle of Fredericksburg just three months later. He was appointed to command the Army of the Potomac in January 1863. Hooker lost to Lee in the Battle of Chancellorsville in May 1863. He was removed from the Army of the Potomac in June 1863, just before the Battle of Gettysburg. Hooker saw combat in the Battle of Chattanooga and the Siege of Atlanta.

- **George Custer (1839–76)** is remembered more for his last stand at Little Bighorn in 1876 than his participation in the Civil War. Custer proved to be an adept and skilled soldier. At 23, he became the youngest general in the Union army. He distinguished himself on the third day of the Battle of Gettysburg, as part of the cavalry force that held off Jeb Stuart and prevented him from supporting Lee's assault on the Union center. Custer and Stuart met again at the Battle of Yellow Tavern, in which Stuart was killed.

The Confederacy

- **Albert Sidney Johnston (1803–62)** was a very skilled commander who was killed during the Battle of Shiloh in April 1862. Johnston was appointed commander of the Confederate Department of the Mississippi when the war broke out, and though undermanned, he managed to establish a bulkhead in Kentucky to protect Tennessee from a Union offensive. He held the position until January 1862, when he was overrun by Grant's superior numbers.

- **Braxton Bragg (1817–76)** was greatly disliked by his superiors as well as those who served under him. Bragg showed flair as a military tactician but also demonstrated potentially fatal indecision on the battlefield. He commanded the coast between Pensacola and Mobile during the first summer of the war and was promoted to major general of the regular army in September 1861. Bragg served under Albert Johnston as chief of staff and participated in the Battle of Shiloh. He was promoted to commander of the Confederate army of the Mississippi in June 1862, replacing Pierre Beauregard. Bragg had initial successes in Kentucky but lost the opportunity for more gains by wasting time trying to set up a secessionist government in Frankfort. He also participated in the Battle of Murfreesboro, the Battle of Chickamauga, and the Battle of Missionary Ridge.

PART TWO

THE ENGAGEMENTS OF WARTIME

TODAY'S SOLDIERS ARE PROFESSIONALS, HIGHLY TRAINED and skilled in everything they do. But things were a lot different during the Civil War. At the beginning of hostilities, the U.S. Army was fairly small (totaling about 15,000 men) and widely spread out, hardly ready to invade and conquer the rebellious South. And the Confederacy was even worse off. As a fledgling nation, it didn't even have a standing army, much less a war machine, nor did it have the weapons to fight even if it wanted to.

34.
A WAR OF AMATEURS

ON BOTH SIDES, THE Civil War was essentially a war of amateurs. For the most part, the commanding officers were trained military men, a great many of them graduates of West Point and veterans of the Mexican War and other military conflicts. But the men serving under them were almost all volunteers, farmers and businessmen who put down their tools, picked up their guns, and marched off to do battle for a cause they believed in: the preservation of their beloved republics.

General Winfield Scott, Lincoln's general-in-chief at the beginning of the Civil War, greatly disliked volunteer soldiers. He had fought with them during the Mexican War and found them to be generally more trouble than they were worth. They were untrained, unskilled, and ill behaved. In short, they were not the type of soldiers he wanted.

However, the Union desperately needed their services; though it had plenty of weapons, it lacked the manpower to engage in a full-scale war. So on April 15, 1861, Lincoln put out a national call for 75,000 militia to sign up for a three-month enlistment, the length of time he felt would be needed to restore order and bring the South back into the Union. The call was met with enthusiasm, and the Union army soon had far more than 75,000 volunteers, eager, if not ready, to fight. In the South, Jefferson Davis enlisted 100,000 men for one year.

General Scott begged for more time to train the volunteer forces (as well as organize the supply services required to keep them armed, fed, and clothed in the battlefield). He knew from experience that, though enthusiastic, few of the new recruits had the skill and training necessary to fight an armed enemy. They would require extensive training in the use of firearms, strategy, and combat, and these were things that couldn't be taught in a day. But while Lincoln may have concurred with Scott in his evaluation of the Union's volunteer militias, he was also facing heavy pressure from Congress, the press, and the public to get matters underway and bring the war to a quick end. As a result, most volunteer soldiers received a minimum of training, if any, before shipping out for battle.

The Confederate army was slightly better off when it came to volunteer soldiers. They, too, received a minimum of drilling and instruction, but because most Confederate soldiers were farmers and outdoorsmen, they tended to be much more skilled with a rifle. They were also fighting on home turf and knew the terrain much better than the invading Union soldiers. This gave the Confederate army a decided home-field advantage.

When the fighting started in earnest, however, the volunteer forces on both sides quickly came to know the bitter taste of fear. It's one thing to be able to pick a squirrel off a tree branch at 50 yards, but it's quite another to fire and advance while other men are shooting at you. Most of their commanding officers had become battle hardened in the Mexican War and other conflicts, but the typical foot soldiers had not. For them, it was literally a trial by fire, and many found warfare more frightening than they ever imagined. In many cases, campfire braggadocio gave way to blind panic in the face of enemy bullets. But those who survived the first battles of the war became better soldiers, and they helped teach and inspire the constant flood of new recruits. In some cases, the volunteers proved to be even better fighters than the soldiers in the regular army, and some officers came to prefer them on the battlefield. Noted General Thomas J. Wood, who commanded a division at the Battle of Chickamauga: "[The volunteers] will 'stick' you; you can fight them as long as you please....The regulars are too sharp. They know when they are whipped but the volunteers don't; they will fight as long as they can pull a trigger."

35.
The Changing Face of Warfare

THE CIVIL WAR WAS the first "modern" war in that it incorporated technological advances that would change the face of combat forever. The use of gunpowder and firearms was introduced into warfare in the fourteenth century, and up until the Civil War, soldiers typically stood like pickets on a fence, shooting at each other across fields with single-shot muskets and other imprecise weapons. It was awkward and time consuming and not particularly effective. But the Civil War changed all that.

Within a year of the war's onset, it became considerably easier to kill or be killed. Unfortunately, many military leaders failed to take these advances into account and used old tactics of attack that put their soldiers in considerable jeopardy from a much more distant enemy. The result was an unexpectedly high number of casualties.

Sign of the Changing Times **The traditional musket, which could take up to a minute to reload even by a skilled soldier, was replaced with a variety of more modern weapons, including breech-loading rifles and carbines that offered greater accuracy, distance, and firepower.**

The Civil War also saw a large number of other unique innovations. The use of trains to ferry soldiers and equipment from one place to another was a historical first, as was the use of the telegraph by commanders in the field to transmit information and stay in touch with their fellow officers. Not surprisingly, a lot of time and energy went into destroying enemy train tracks and telegraph wires.

In naval combat, the most important innovation of the Civil War was the creation and use of ironclad ships. In the past, warships were all made of wood, which was very susceptible to enemy artillery. In comparison, the ironclads, while somewhat unwieldy, were practically indestructible. The two-hour battle between the Union ironclad *Monitor* and the Confederate ironclad *Virginia* (formerly the *Merrimac*) outside of Norfolk Harbor in March 1862 is a prime example of how sturdy the ships could be. Hundreds of shots were fired from both ships, but when the smoke cleared, neither ship had been penetrated or seriously damaged. Both sides claimed victory, but in truth, the duel had been a draw—and clear evidence that naval warfare would never be the same.

Of course, this is far from a complete analysis. There were hundreds of small skirmishes and minor battles between the major battlefield events.

36.
THE FUNDING
OF THE WAR

BOTH SIDES POURED MILLIONS of dollars into their war machines, with the citizens of the Union and the Confederacy ultimately taking the brunt through ever-increasing taxes.

Most people believe a federal income tax is a relatively new phenomenon, but in truth, it was first enacted by the Secretary of the Treasury, Salmon B. Chase, as a way of funding the war effort. In the beginning, money was provided through loans from private financiers, then war bonds marketed by Philadelphia banker Jay Cooke, which brought the government more than a billion dollars. When the sources of private capital disappeared, Chase was allowed to print a national currency under the Legal Tender Act. The money, known as greenbacks, was backed by treasury gold. (Previously, each state had printed its own money.)

Congress passed the first Internal Revenue Act at the same time it passed the Legal Tender Act. This was necessary because the government's international credit rating had plummeted as a result of early Northern defeats (no one wanted to fund a loser), and money for the war effort, which was costing an estimated $2.5 million a day by 1862, was growing tight. The first income tax rates were just 3 percent, but the government also enacted other taxes as well, including a sin tax on tobacco and liquor, a luxury tax on jewels and other items, and a license tax. In short, the government dug deep into the pockets of its citizenry in a desperate attempt to keep its war machine going.

Funding for the war was even more difficult for the Confederacy. Christopher Memminger, a South Carolinian of German descent, was appointed the first secretary of the treasury and ordered to find a way to keep the war funds coming. At first, lacking the internal organization to establish taxes or tariffs, Memminger turned to the sale of war bonds, which could be redeemed when the war was over. The bonds sold briskly following the capture of Fort Sumter, but sales dried up as it became increasingly evident that the effort was doomed, and soon they were worthless.

Sign of the Changing Times Ultimately, its failure to get funding from overseas forced the Confederate government to tap its citizens, who found themselves paying a series of taxes that made those imposed by the federal government look positively friendly. In addition, to a federal income tax, the Confederacy also required a 10 percent "tax in kind," which required farmers to turn over to the government a portion of all the crops they grew.

37.
FORT SUMTER
FALLS

APRIL 12–13, 1861. It could be said that the Civil War officially started with the Confederate attack on Fort Sumter in Charleston Harbor, South Carolina. It was a relatively one-sided "battle" because the Union fort was low on men and supplies, but it signaled to the world that the South meant business in its conflict with the North.

When Abraham Lincoln was inaugurated, he vowed that the federal government would not start a war with the South, nor would it try to take back federal facilities held at that point by Confederate forces. He did promise, however, to "hold, occupy, and possess" forts and other installations still under federal control within the Confederacy, and that included Fort Sumter.

Lincoln was thrown into the first serious crisis of his presidency the day after his inauguration, when he received a frantic wire from Major Robert Anderson, the commander of Fort Sumter, stating that the facility had less than a six-week supply of food. The fort would be impossible to hold if new supplies were not sent immediately.

General-in-Chief Winfield Scott told Lincoln that re-supplying the fort would be impossible, and Secretary of State William Seward advised that it simply be evacuated in an attempt to cool growing hostilities in South Carolina, which had been the first state to secede from the Union. Lincoln chose an option he hoped would appease both sides: He would re-supply the fort but not reinforce its defenses. He then sent a message to Francis Pickens, the governor of South Carolina, telling him of his decision.

Jefferson Davis, however, was not in a conciliatory mood. He wanted nothing less than the surrender of the fort, the presence of which he saw as an insult to the Confederacy, and ordered Beauregard to take it by force if necessary. Beauregard sent Anderson a message informing him of his intent to bombard the fort if it were not evacuated, to which a pragmatic Anderson replied, "Gentlemen, I will await the first shot and if you do not batter the fort to pieces about us, we shall be starved out in a few days." Anderson then informed Beauregard's emissary that he would evacuate the fort by noon on April 15 if he did not receive additional orders or supplies by that time. Anderson was told the terms were not acceptable.

On April 12, at 4:30 A.M., a single mortar was fired to signal the 43 Confederate guns around Fort Sumter to begin their assault. More than 4,000 shells were fired at the fort, but amazingly, no one within was injured. On the second day of the bombardment, hot shells set portions of the fort on fire. Realizing there was no way he could mount any type of reasonable defense, Anderson ordered the American flag lowered and replaced it with a white flag of surrender.

During the fort's evacuation the next day, Anderson ordered a cannon salute to the flag. During the ceremony, one of the big guns exploded, killing Private Daniel Hough. Another soldier, Private Edward Galloway, was gravely injured in the explosion and died a few days later. They were the war's first military casualties, victims of an accident.

On April 15, Abraham Lincoln proclaimed a state of insurrection rather than a state of war and issued a call for 75,000 volunteers to quell the rebellion. The Civil War had officially begun.

38.
BULL RUN,
PART 1

JULY 21, 1861. The First Battle of Bull Run was the first real battle of the war. Union officials felt it would be an easy victory and would lead to a quick conclusion to the war, but history proved otherwise. At the end, the Confederacy was the winner, routing inexperienced Union forces and sending them fleeing all the way back to Washington.

The battle was set more for political than military reasons. Confederate leaders were eager to prove their mettle against the more industrial North and announced their intentions to move the capital of the Confederacy to Richmond, Virginia, a situation that greatly angered Northern politicians. Meanwhile, the press and the public were loudly pushing for the Union to move "on to Richmond" and end the war as quickly as possible. More importantly, by the time the battle was set, many of the 75,000 volunteer recruits were nearing the end of their 90-day enlistment and were getting ready to go home.

Union General Irvin McDowell's strategy for the battle was simple: His plan was to invade Virginia, crush the Confederate forces, and push on to Richmond. Opposing him in this endeavor was Confederate General Pierre G. T. Beauregard, already a Confederate war hero as a result of his role in the fall of Fort Sumter. If the Confederacy could win the first battle of the war, Beauregard reasoned, it might impress upon the Union the strength and fortitude of the Confederate army and result in a truce that in turn might lead to an early peace.

Each side was divided into three armies. McDowell had 30,600 troops along the Potomac facing 20,000 Confederate soldiers under Beauregard, who had amassed his forces behind a creek called Bull Run near Manassas Junction. Union General Robert Patterson had 18,000 men facing 12,000 Confederates under Joseph E. Johnston near Harpers Ferry. And Union General Benjamin Butler commanded 10,000 men in Fort Monroe at the tip of the Virginia peninsula, guarded by a small unit of Confederates under John B. Magruder (neither Butler nor Magruder would play a role in Bull Run).

McDowell's first objective was to attack Beauregard and drive him from Manassas Junction by feigning an attack on the Confederate center, then clobbering the Confederate left. He ordered Patterson to keep Johnston busy at Harpers Ferry so that Johnston couldn't join Beauregard, thus giving McDowell a decided advantage in numbers. However, Johnston gave Patterson the slip and was able to come to Beauregard's aid, as did others.

McDowell left Washington for Manassas Junction on July 16, 1861. But his army was large and slow, due primarily to a huge number of supply wagons and the carefree attitude of the neophyte soldiers, who often broke rank to gather berries or rest in the shade, and he didn't arrive until July 18. On that day, Union reconnaissance troops sent to feel out the enemy were met and driven back by Confederate forces at Blackburn's Ford; it was a small Confederate victory that demoralized the green Union troops.

The battle itself began on July 21. Beauregard's grand plan to attack McDowell, based on Napoleon's strategy at Austerlitz, was a dismal and immediate failure because of the inexperience of his troops. McDowell's army gained an early advantage thanks to its greater numbers, and it appeared the Union would win; several Confederate units were defeated as Union infantry advanced on a small plateau called Henry House Hill (it was here that Stonewall Jackson was given his famous nickname).

But just when a Union victory seemed assured, Johnston's army arrived from Harpers Ferry to reinforce Beauregard's army.

On the Homefront **Fighting aggressively, the Confederate forces caused the Union line to crumble. Retreat was called, and the Union soldiers, most of whom had never been in battle before, began to race to the rear as the Confederates shot at them.**

The retreat turned into a rout as officers abandoned their troops, terrified soldiers fled in panic, and the entire Union supply train became a horrible, tangled mess of carts, trucks, and ambulances. Chaos reigned, and the situation was made worse by the presence of hundreds of sightseers, many with picnic baskets in hand, who had arrived from Washington in carriages and buggies, to watch from a grassy slope a few miles away what was assumed to be a forgone Union victory. It would have been comical if it hadn't been so tragic. Federal losses totaled 2,896 men dead, wounded, or missing. Confederate losses totaled 1,982.

The First Battle of Bull Run would foreshadow a great many other battles in which outmanned and outgunned Confederate forces would defeat the Union army through skill, bravery, and sheer battlefield tenacity. It also proved to Lincoln and others that the short, clean war they had hoped for was not going to happen.

39.
SHILOH, BLOODY
SHILOH

APRIL 6–7, 1862. This battle, the bloodiest of the war up until that date, is considered an important Union victory, though Ulysses S. Grant was greatly criticized for his efforts. The Union originally called this engagement the Battle of Pittsburg Landing, after the Tennessee River embankment the Union forces were defending, but both sides eventually named it Shiloh, after the Methodist log meeting house near the site.

Grant was stationed with 42,000 troops on the west side of the Tennessee River near the Mississippi border. He remained there for nearly a month, waiting for the arrival of Don Carlos Buell's army. Their combined forces were to head south to attack an important Confederate railroad center called Corinth, which was being protected by Confederate General Albert Sidney Johnston. However, Johnston decided to attack first, hoping to catch Grant's troops before Buell arrived. Johnston's second in command, Pierre G. T. Beauregard, liked the idea at first but then changed his mind; he felt that 20,000 soldiers on a 20-mile march would be too easily detected and that Grant would be reinforced before they arrived.

But when Johnston's army arrived at Pittsburg Landing on April 6, they found no signs of Buell's arrival. The Confederate forces caught the Union troops off guard (Grant was away from the front receiving treatment for an injured leg), and after three hours of brutal, bloody fighting, they managed to overrun the divisions commanded by William T. Sherman and Benjamin Prentiss near Shiloh Church. The battle could have turned into a rout, but Johnston's army lost its momentum when his soldiers started rummaging through the now-abandoned Union camps looking for food and supplies.

The battle became increasingly disorganized, and soldiers on both sides scrambled to find their correct units. One major battle turned into numerous smaller skirmishes, with both sides taking heavy casualties. In many cases, confused Confederate troops dressed in both blue and gray fired on their own men, and hundreds of panic-stricken soldiers on both sides ran from the battlefield in terror.

When Grant arrived on the scene, he ordered his remaining men to hold their positions in a dense thicket at all costs. With Grant barking orders and doing his best to rally them, the Union soldiers managed to repel more than a dozen hard Confederate charges. Johnston, who was directing the assaults, took a bullet in the foot and bled to death at 2:30 P.M. Three hours later, the 2,200 defenders of the thicket, which came to be known as "the Hornet's Nest" because of the constant gunfire, were ordered to surrender as they came under fire from Confederate artillery. But it was growing dark, and it had started to rain, so Beauregard, who assumed command upon Johnston's death, decided to delay a final assault until the next morning. The decision would cost him greatly.

During the night, Grant was greatly reinforced by Don Carlos Buell's army, and Beauregard awakened the following morning to face an army nearly twice as strong as before. Fighting resumed around 7:30 A.M. and the Union forces were able to recapture almost all of the ground they had lost the day before. The Confederates made one counterattack but were pushed back. Late in the afternoon, Beauregard ordered a withdrawal back to Corinth, covered by Nathan Forrest's cavalry.

More than 13,000 Union soldiers were killed, wounded, or missing in the battle, compared to 10,694 on the Confederate side; this loss was more than twice the number of dead in all previous engagements combined.

Sign of the Changing Times **Grant's army won the battle, but Grant was strongly rebuked for being caught by surprise. His superior officer, Henry Halleck, accused Grant of being drunk at the time (an accusation that was not true, but was typical of Halleck) and also blamed him for the large number of Union casualties.**

40.
ANTIETAM, THE SINGLE BLOODIEST DAY

SEPTEMBER 17, 1862. The Battle of Antietam was the single bloodiest day of fighting in the Civil War, with a combined total of about 23,000 casualties. It was also a decisive victory for the Union and gave Abraham Lincoln the confidence he needed to issue his Emancipation Proclamation, which effectively changed the Union's war aims to include the abolition of slavery and increased manpower by allowing black soldiers to participate.

Prior to Antietam, Robert E. Lee, riding high on the Confederate victory at the Second Battle of Bull Run, planned an invasion of the North through western Maryland. Lee's primary goal was the capture of the Union railroad center in Harrisburg, Pennsylvania. He hoped to take the town by dividing his army. While he moved into Pennsylvania, Stonewall Jackson would capture the Union garrison at Harpers Ferry, then hook up with Major General James Longstreet's three divisions and join Lee near Harrisburg.

The plan might have worked, considering Union commander George McClellan's hesitancy to strike in the face of what he thought were superior numbers. But, through an incredible quirk of fate, McClellan came into possession of a copy of Lee's plans, which had been found wrapped around some cigars near an abandoned Confederate camp. However, McClellan considered that the orders might be a trap and failed to act on them for nearly 16 hours.

Lee, meanwhile, was informed that his plans were now in the hands of the enemy and worked hard to protect his three vulnerable flanks. But fighting broke out in a number of locations along the planned route, and the Confederates experienced heavy casualties. On September 15, Lee was planning a retreat back into Virginia when he learned that Jackson had taken Harpers Ferry and collected some much-needed supplies. Lee quickly changed his mind and ordered all of his divisions to meet in Sharpsburg. McClellan, again overly cautious, allowed Lee's forces to converge. On September 17, he finally attacked; 75,000 Union troops faced just 40,000 Confederates.

Lee's left flank, led by Stonewall Jackson, was almost annihilated during the Union onslaught, led by Joseph Hooker, Joseph Mansfield, and Edwin Sumner. The rebel soldiers took a horrible pounding until they were reinforced by two fresh Confederate divisions, who fought back with amazing vigor. Within just 20 minutes, an astounding 2,200 Union soldiers were killed or wounded in an area known as the West Woods, and Sumner was forced to retreat.

Later in the day, the Union army focused on decimating the Confederate center, led by Major General Daniel Hill. Sumner's remaining divisions attacked Hill's line for three brutal hours, resulting in such carnage that the narrow street on which it occurred became known as Bloody Lane. The assault broke the Confederate center, and Union forces under the command of General Ambrose Burnside crossed Antietam Creek to attack Lee's right flank. Lee's army probably would have been destroyed during the ensuing battle if it hadn't been reinforced by a division led by A. P. Hill, which arrived after a grueling 30-mile march from Harpers Ferry. Upon arrival, Hill's men launched a blistering counterattack that helped keep the Union forces at bay.

Had McClellan continued his assault, it's very likely that he could have completely devastated Lee's army. But instead of making one final push, he let his troops rest, as did Lee. Lee retreated back to Virginia on the evening of September 18, having lost nearly a quarter of his army at Antietam.

MAY 1–4, 1863. Many historians consider the Battle of Chancellors-

41.
LEE'S GREATEST VICTORY: CHANCELLORSVILLE

ville to be one of Lee's greatest victories. Greatly outnumbered, he out-planned and outmaneuvered his opponent so skillfully that Hooker never knew what hit him. This victory helped the South make some strategic gains in the eastern theater and put the Union on the defensive.

Conflict of Interest **Lincoln was looking for a skilled commander who would aggressively pursue Lee's army, and Hooker, who was arrogant and vain but well liked by his men, had fought well in the Peninsula campaign and at the Battle of Antietam and showed tremendous promise.**

Joseph Hooker replaced Ambrose E. Burnside as commander of the Army of the Potomac on Lincoln's orders, following the Union's winter defeat in Fredericksburg and the embarrassing "Mud March" that resulted.

Hooker, shortly before a planned offensive against the Confederate general near Fredericksburg, wrote a letter to the president in which he stated, "May God have mercy on General Lee, for I will have none."

Hooker arrived in Chancellorsville, at a house in the middle of a clearing about 10 miles west of Fredericksburg, on April 27 and set up camp. He was confident that he could destroy Lee's army with overwhelming numbers but failed to take into consideration Lee's considerable skills as a strategist. With just 60,000 troops at his disposal, Lee used the same tactic that brought victory at the Second Battle of Bull Run: He divided his troops, leaving 10,000 men at Fredericksburg and taking the rest to defend his vulnerable flank.

The armies first clashed on May 1. Hooker's men were climbing through dense woods (nicknamed the Wilderness) toward the Confederate line when they were met with a surprise attack by Stonewall Jackson. Startled, Hooker lost his nerve and, against the advice of his commanders, immediately ordered a withdrawal into the woods. Major General Jeb Stuart notified Lee that Hooker's right flank was vulnerable, so Lee divided his forces yet again, ordering Jackson to attack with 26,000 men.

Hooker had been advised of Jackson's movements by scouts, but he didn't think Jackson posed much of a threat and failed to act. As the sun was about to set on the evening of May 2, Jackson and his men attacked troops under General Oliver O. Howard. The soldiers were caught completely unaware and forced into a two-mile withdrawal before Union artillery stopped Jackson just short of the Chancellorsville house.

It was a grand victory for Lee's outnumbered army, but there was little celebrating because Stonewall Jackson had been shot in both arms by some of his own men as he returned to camp in the approaching darkness. Jackson's left arm was amputated in a desperate move to save him, but he died of pneumonia a few days later. Jeb Stuart assumed command of the infantry and launched another attack against Hooker's army on the morning of May 3, pushing them all the way back to the Rappahannock and Rapidan.

As Stuart attacked Hooker, Lee found that his rear was being threatened by Union troops led by Major General John Sedgwick. On May 4, a portion of Lee's army in Fredericksburg attacked Sedgwick's forces at Salem Church, engaging in a brutal day-long battle that ultimately pushed Sedgwick across the Rappahannock. Hooker joined Sedgwick in his retreat the following day, giving the Confederate army an amazing win against overwhelming odds— and the Union a humiliating defeat that never should have occurred, considering it held the advantage in sheer manpower. The Union army suffered more than 17,000 casualties in the relatively brief engagement; the Confederacy lost about 13,000. Joseph Hooker was removed from command of the Army of the Potomac a month later.

42.
BLOOD BATH
AT GETTYSBURG

JULY 1–3, 1863. The three-day battle is perhaps the best remembered clash of the entire Civil War. It was a literal bloodbath, with both sides taking heavy casualties (a combined total of more than 50,000 men dead, wounded, missing, or captured), and it put a quick end to the second (and final) Confederate invasion of the North.

The Confederate army greatly outnumbered the Union forces during the first day of fighting and used their advantage to drive Union troops led by Major General Winfield Scott Hancock through the town of Gettysburg to Cemetery Ridge, which lay to the south. The Confederates might have enjoyed a tremendous victory had they engaged in one last assault on the hills, but General Richard Ewell decided not to attempt another attack because nightfall was approaching.

After three days, Lee ordered an attack on the center of the Union line by approximately 11,000 fresh soldiers under the command of Major General George Pickett and others. It was then that Jeb Stuart finally returned, and Lee ordered him to attack the Union rear with his cavalry.

On the Homefront   The last battle of the vicious, bloody engagement started at 1 P.M. with a deafening artillery duel. The cannons roared, and at 3:30 P.M., Pickett and his men started a charge against Union forces at Cemetery Ridge.

The charge was pure suicide; Pickett's men marched across an open field, only to be slaughtered by Union artillery that had been held in reserve. A handful of men made the crossing successfully and managed to capture a short stretch of the Union line, but they were unable to hold it.

Jeb Stuart's assault on the Union rear flank, which lasted nearly three hours, was equally unsuccessful. Despite his best efforts, Stuart was unable to make much headway, and he, too, suffered heavy casualties. By the end of the day, Lee knew he had been defeated and decided to pull his army back into Virginia. Unable to carry his wounded, Lee left nearly 7,000 injured soldiers in Union care. Had Union forces pursued him in his retreat the following day, they might have been able to completely disable the Confederate war machine and bring the conflict to a quick close. However, Meade and his men were exhausted, and he opted to let Lee go. As a result, the war would endure for another two years. A month after his defeat at Gettysburg, Lee offered his resignation to Jefferson Davis. Davis refused to accept it.

43.
THE ROCK OF
CHICKAMAUGA

SEPTEMBER 19–20, 1863. The Battle of Chickamauga, named after a creek in northwest Georgia, proved to be the region's bloodiest engagement. It was an important Confederate victory that nearly destroyed the Union's war effort in the western theater.

Over the previous month, the Army of the Cumberland, under the command of Major General William Rosecrans, had engaged in a successful campaign that concluded with the occupation of Chattanooga, Tennessee, an important gateway to the southeastern region of the Confederacy. Rosecrans was eager to press his foe, Confederate General Braxton Bragg, who commanded the Army of Tennessee, but he fell victim to misinformation that the Confederate troops were retreating and quickly sent his army in pursuit. In truth, Bragg was gathering reinforcements in northern Georgia with the goal of retaking Chattanooga. When James Longstreet arrived, Bragg's forces outnumbered Rosecrans's by nearly 10,000 men.

Worse for Rosecrans, he had to divide his army into three columns during its advance through the treacherous terrain around the city. They would have made easy pickings for Bragg's army, but delays and poor planning kept Bragg's subordinates from launching an effective attack, and several small skirmishes alerted Rosecrans to Bragg's trap.

On September 13, Rosecrans began regrouping his troops on the west bank of Chickamauga Creek, just across the Georgia border. Patrols from both sides engaged in a number of small skirmishes near the creek on September 18, and the Battle of Chickamauga began with a vengeance the next day.

Bragg's strategy was to attack Rosecrans's left flank and smash the Union army by forcing it into a valley from which it could not retreat back to Chattanooga. However, assaults by Confederate troops were met with a withering response from soldiers commanded by George Henry Thomas. The day's fighting in the area's thick woods degenerated into vicious hand-to-hand combat that brought the Confederates only very small gains and heavy casualties on both sides.

Confederate Lieutenant General Leonidas Polk was instructed to perform a sideways attack against Thomas early on September 20, but Polk delayed the assault. Bragg then ordered Longstreet to conduct an all-out frontal attack, which proved very successful. Rosecrans, unable to see a large section of his troops, erroneously believed there was a break in his lines and sent an entire division to fill it, leaving a gap on the Union right. Longstreet's forces barreled through the weakened Union line, overrunning Rosecrans's headquarters and forcing more than half of his army into a retreat back to Chattanooga.

Rosecrans himself was swept up in the retreat, leaving George Henry Thomas to command what was left of the Union force. Thomas bravely refused to retreat and rallied his troops to form a defensible line on the ridge of Snodgrass Hill. For the remainder of the day, Longstreet and Polk sent wave after wave against the Union forces, but they were unable to dislodge them. As a result of his stalwart defense, Thomas received the nickname "The Rock of Chickamauga."

Thomas finally realized the futility of his position and ordered his men to withdraw back to Chattanooga as night fell. The Confederates were handed a victory, but Thomas's bravery in the face of overwhelming odds helped keep the Union army from being completely destroyed as it retreated. Nonetheless, the casualties on both sides were enormous. More than 16,000 Union soldiers were killed, wounded, missing, or captured, and more than 18,500 Confederate soldiers—nearly 30 percent of the troops involved in the battle—met similar fates. The Confederate dead or wounded included ten of Bragg's generals, a situation that so depressed him that he failed to attack the Union forces in retreat toward Chattanooga. Bragg's inaction, which allowed the Union forces to regroup and fortify in Chattanooga, greatly angered his subordinates; Longstreet and Polk demanded that he be dismissed, and Nathan Bedford Forrest refused to serve under him any longer.

But despite Bragg's failure to strike a decisive blow against the Union army, the Confederate victory at Chickamauga did wonders to revive the flagging spirits of the South, which had suffered greatly as a result of defeats at Gettysburg and Vicksburg.

44.
CHATTANOOGA, ONE MORE NAIL IN THE COFFIN

OCTOBER–NOVEMBER 1863. The Union forces were able to hold off Confederate assaults on their fortification in Chattanooga, so Confederate General Braxton Bragg ordered a siege. Supply lines to the city were severed in early October, and within weeks, the entrenched Union soldiers found themselves perilously low on food and other supplies.

To the rescue was Major General Ulysses S. Grant, recently appointed commander of the Military Division of the Mississippi. Grant replaced William Rosecrans with Major General George Thomas as commander of the Army of the Cumberland, then, with his chief engineer, William F. Smith, he developed a daring plan to break the Confederate siege. The first part of his strategy was to open a supply line by attacking Confederate forces on the east bank of the Tennessee River, then establishing a bridgehead at Brown's Ferry. Supplies could then be shipped by boat to Brown's Ferry and transported across Moccasin Point to the waiting troops in Chattanooga.

Grant was able to force the Confederates off Raccoon Mountain and put his so-called "cracker line operation" into effect on October 26. Confederate forces assaulted the new line at Wauhatchie on October 28 and 29, but the first supply ship still arrived safely on November 1. As he waited for reinforcements to arrive from Memphis and Vicksburg, Grant planned the next step of his offensive: He must force the Confederates off their dangerous position on Missionary Ridge, along the northeastern and southeastern sides of Chattanooga, and from Lookout Mountain on the southwestern side.

At the same time that Grant was forming his strategy, the Confederate army underwent some dramatic changes. Lieutenant General Leonidas Polk, Daniel H. Hill, and Thomas C. Hindman, disgusted with Bragg's slowness at Chattanooga, complained to the War Department and were granted transfers. Bragg also picked this time to send several divisions and 35 cannon under the command of Lieutenant General James Longstreet eastward to help troops in West Virginia in their campaign against Union General Ambrose Burnside. This move severely weakened his lines on Missionary Ridge just as the Union army was getting ready for a major assault.

Grant's plan went into action on November 23 with the arrival of fresh troops under the command of William T. Sherman. Grant's first goal was Orchard Knob, which was the forward position in the center of the Confederate line on Missionary Ridge. The battle began with an ingenious ruse on Grant's part: He dressed his divisions as if for a military parade and had them march below the hill. When curious Confederate soldiers on the knob moved down for a closer look, the Union soldiers attacked and, following a heated battle, took control of the hill.

Grant made Orchard Hill his headquarters for the coming fight and ordered Sherman's divisions to cross the Tennessee River and attack the

Confederate right on the north end of Missionary Ridge. He also ordered Hooker to take Lookout Mountain on the Confederate left. Early on the morning of November 24, Hooker engaged the enemy in a battle made difficult by rain and fog; hours later, he emerged the victor. Sherman, delayed by the rain, made slower progress and didn't arrive on Bragg's right until that afternoon.

As Sherman approached, Bragg ordered half of his troops to the bottom of the hill with instructions to fire a volley when the Union army was within 200 yards and then withdraw up the slopes. But Bragg wasn't known for his outstanding communication skills, and he failed to inform all of his men of the plan.

The Battle of Missionary Ridge began on the morning of November 25. Sherman's forces and artillery struck repeatedly at the Confederate line along the north end, but they were repelled. To draw the Confederates away from Sherman's front, Grant ordered Thomas to attack the Confederate forces at the base of the ridge. The wiser Confederate soldiers realized what was happening and withdrew immediately, but many stayed and fought, only to be overrun by Union troops. Having taken the Confederate line, the Union soldiers, acting without orders, decided to pay back the Confederates for the Union defeat at Chickamauga by racing up the mountain slope in an unexpected attack that successfully drove the rebels into a full retreat. Chattanooga was saved.

The defeat at Chattanooga was an important nail in the coffin of the Confederate cause. It cost the South important communication and supply lines and opened the door for Sherman's Atlanta campaign.

45.
LEE AND GRANT
MEET IN THE
WILDERNESS

MAY 5–7, 1864. The Battle of the Wilderness in Virginia's Rapidan basin was the first battle between Ulysses S. Grant and Robert E. Lee and was the beginning of a 40-day campaign that would include some of the bloodiest fighting of the entire war. Grant, who had been appointed general-in-chief of the Union army, had one thing on his mind: a final battle between Meade's Army of the Potomac and Lee's Army of Northern Virginia that, he hoped, would be instrumental in bringing the Confederacy to its knees.

Union troops started crossing the Rapidan River and heading south to confront Confederate forces near the site of the Battle of Chancellorsville. In order to reach their destination, the Union army had to pass through the dense forest known as the Wilderness, where Lee had won a decided victory almost exactly a year earlier. As Grant's troops trudged through the forest and brush, they came across countless reminders of that previous battle, including bleached bones, firearms, and other debris. It was Grant's hope that his men could clear the Wilderness before engaging Lee.

On the Homefront The forest was so thick that soldiers on both sides became entangled and separated from regiments, and entire units found themselves completely lost. Visibility was also severely hampered by the thick underbrush and smoke from brushfires ignited by bursting shells. Chaos reigned as frightened soldiers soon started shooting at anything that moved in the thickets, often hitting their own men.

However, Lee had other plans. He realized the value of the Wilderness and planned to use it to his advantage, since his army was outmanned 115,000 to 60,000. The battle started on May 5 when Union and Confederate troops accidentally found each other while the Union soldiers were still crossing the forest. Both sides quickly called for reinforcements, and around 1 P.M., the Union army prepared a major assault.

As Lee had hoped, the familiar terrain gave the Confederate soldiers a strong advantage over their Union counterparts. However, the Union forces had far more men and were able to absorb greater casualties while continuing to fight. Grant ordered assault after assault against the Confederate lines, all of which were repelled with heavy casualties on both sides. But by the end of the first day of fighting, Grant had succeeded in weakening Lee's right flank, which he hoped to destroy with one more major attack.

At dawn the following day, Union forces began hammering the Confederate center, pushing their way forward until they were almost on top of Lee's field headquarters. But by this time, Lee had received much-needed reinforcements from James Longstreet and others, and a counterattack was mounted, to be led by John Gregg, who had assumed command of Hood's

Texas Brigade. Lee himself wanted to lead the charge, but the Texas troops refused to budge until Lee was safely behind the lines.

Longstreet's troops, fresh and rested, managed to push back the Union forces through much of the morning, and a massive attack on the Union's left flank was put in motion. However, the momentum of the moment was broken when Longstreet was accidentally wounded by one of his own men. By the time Lee was able to coordinate a new assault later that afternoon, the Union forces had regrouped and were able to successfully defend themselves.

At the same time, a late attack on the Union's right, led by Confederate commander John Gordon, was able to drive the Union army back one mile, though the federal soldiers quickly reclaimed all the land they had lost and were almost back in position by nightfall. However, the temporary setback demoralized Grant's headquarters.

Neither Grant nor Lee was particularly happy with the way the battle had gone. The Union experienced more than twice the casualties as the Confederacy (17,500 to 7,750), but Lee hadn't gained much ground.

The two armies went at it again the following morning with a number of small skirmishes. Lee had expected Grant to retreat, considering the fact that he had assumed such heavy losses and gained little in the bargain, but Grant was resolute. Rather than pull back, he ordered an advance, his plan now being for George Meade's army to move south past Lee's right and position itself between Lee's army and the Confederate capital of Richmond. The Battle of the Wilderness ended in a tactical draw, only to resume a day later in the small crossroads town of Spotsylvania Court House.

46.
COUNTERCHARGE AT SPOTSYLVANIA

MAY 8–19, 1864. Following the Battle of the Wilderness, which concluded with a heavy loss of life and not much else for either side, Grant ordered his men to advance further south in the hope of blocking Lee's path back to Richmond. Lee anticipated this move and raced south too, arriving at Spotsylvania ahead of Grant and with sufficient time to build protective fieldworks. This forced Grant to take the offensive, and he promised to "fight it out on this line if it takes all summer."

Grant first tried an unsuccessful assault on Lee's left flank, then ordered an attack on an area known as the "Mule Shoe," located near the center of the Confederate line. Supported by a heavy artillery barrage, a Union division commanded by Colonel Emory Upton made a running charge late in the day on May 10, breaking through the enemy defense and capturing an astounding number of Confederate prisoners before being driven back.

Grant was pleased with the results of this attack and ordered a larger assault on the center of the Confederate line two days later. Hoping to catch the Confederate forces by surprise, 15,000 men led by Winfield Scott Hancock stormed the enemy line at 4:30 A.M. on May 12, capturing almost an entire infantry division and splitting Lee's army down the middle. The Confederates were no match for Hancock's corps and were pushed back almost half a mile as the Union forces rested and regrouped in trenches formerly occupied by gray-clad rebels.

Lee assembled a countercharge and planned to lead it himself, but cooler minds prevailed upon him to remain safely behind the line. (Had Lee led the charge as he wanted to, history suggests he probably would have been killed in battle.) The two armies met in a battle that lasted more than 20 hours and involved some of the bloodiest hand-to-hand combat seen in modern warfare. Ground, soaked by rain and blood, was won and lost by the foot, with enormous casualties on both sides. As the hours passed, the soggy battlefield literally became covered with the bodies of the dead and wounded. The gunfire was so intense during portions of the battle that trees two feet thick were shorn in half by flying bullets.

Both sides fought with all they had, refusing to give an inch until after midnight, when Lee finally ordered his bone-weary troops to fall back to a new line of freshly dug protective earthworks. Grant tried to flank Lee's army over the next few days, but he met with little success. On May 18, he attempted another frontal assault that did little but kill still more Union soldiers. The following day, May 19, Lee took the offensive and mounted a daring assault on Grant's right. Grant's troops managed to hold their ground, and Grant finally accepted the fact that he would not be able to bring Lee into the open at that time. The next day, he ordered the Army of the Potomac to move south to Hanover Junction, Virginia, forcing Lee's Army of Northern

Virginia to again race ahead in the hope of establishing a line of defense at the next point of engagement. Neither army had much time to rest before the fighting began anew.

The Battle of Spotsylvania took a huge toll on both sides. More than 17,500 Union soldiers were killed, wounded, missing, or captured, and nearly 10,000 Confederate soldiers were also taken out of action. But while the Confederate numbers may have been smaller, they had a more dramatic impact because the South's forces were diminishing rapidly.

47
ATLANTA BURNS

MAY 1–SEPTEMBER 2, 1864. The fall of Atlanta after a four-month campaign and siege was a devastating blow to the South and signaled the end of the war in the western theater. Once Atlanta was under Union control, Sherman set out on his infamous march to the sea and then into the Carolinas, destroying anything he felt could be used to sustain the Confederate war effort. This strategy, combined with Grant's campaign against Lee's Army of Northern Virginia, would ultimately lead to a Confederate surrender. But getting to that point wasn't easy.

Atlanta was vital to Confederate manufacturing and communications, and Sherman knew that taking the city would be a huge step toward ending the conflict. His policy was all-out war, which meant anything that could be used against the North would have to be eliminated. Facing Sherman's 100,000 man army was Confederate General Joseph Johnston, who commanded a considerably smaller army of 62,000 men. Johnston knew he wouldn't stand a chance if he faced Sherman directly, so he tried a different strategy: He planned to keep Sherman away from Atlanta as long as possible, at least until the November elections. If Lincoln were defeated, he reasoned, a new president, tired of the war, might decide to bring hostilities to an end and broker a lasting peace. In the beginning of May, Johnston's army was firmly entrenched along Rocky Face Ridge, a rock wall surrounding a canyon leading into Chattanooga.

After several weeks of fighting, Sherman refused to give up and continued to push Johnston's smaller army, forcing it back bit by bit until Johnston was just seven miles from Atlanta. He later withdrew south of the Chattahoochie River, the last natural barrier between Sherman's army and Atlanta.

Hood leapt into the fray with everything he had, launching a major offensive on July 20 against Sherman's army, which had been split at Peachtree Creek. Hood's men fought bravely, but they were simply

Sign of the Changing Times **Confederate President Jefferson Davis was disappointed with Johnston's tactics and, looking for someone more aggressive and willing to fight, replaced Johnston with Major General John B. Hood.**

outnumbered. More than 4,800 Confederate soldiers were killed or wounded in the ill-fated assault, and Hood was forced to retreat to Atlanta.

Sherman mistakenly believed that Hood had abandoned Atlanta, and he sent McPherson to the south and east of the city to attack Hood in retreat. On July 22, William Hardee's infantry division, hoping to catch Sherman by surprise, attacked Sherman's forces in what became the Battle of Atlanta. But once again the Confederate forces were outmanned and outgunned, losing more than 8,500 men. Union losses during the battle were lighter, but Sherman lost a valued corps commander with the death of James McPherson.

Sherman replaced McPherson with Major General Oliver Howard and sent him around the western side of Atlanta with orders to sever Hood's communication lines. Hood fought back on July 28 with a heated battle at Ezra Church. He successfully protected the railroad there, which was an essential supply line, but he lost another 2,500 men in the process. At this point, the Confederate army numbered fewer than 45,000 men. Facing overwhelming numbers, they fell back behind Atlanta's defensive lines and waited for Sherman to attack.

Sherman laid siege on Atlanta, bombarding the city with heavy artillery for more than a month and doing all he could to destroy its supply lines. But the South refused to give in that easily; Confederate cavalry commander Joseph Wheeler skillfully kept many supply lines in operation until the end of August.

The standoff came to a head on August 28, when Sherman attacked the Montgomery & Atlanta Railroad south of Atlanta. Hood, realizing the importance of keeping the line open, attacked the Union flank at nearby

Jonesborough but ultimately lost after a valiant battle. With no remaining line of defense, Confederate forces evacuated Atlanta on September 2, and Sherman's troops marched in the following day.

The once proud city of Atlanta had been all but destroyed during the siege and final evacuation.

48.
THE BATTLE OF NASHVILLE CLOSES THE WESTERN FRONT

DECEMBER 15–16, 1864. The Battle of Nashville proved to be the undoing of Confederate General John B. Hood and his Army of Tennessee. It brought to a close the major fighting in the war's western theater.

Hood had experienced a devastating defeat at Franklin, about 75 miles south of Nashville, on November 30, but he refused to retreat from Tennessee. He clung to the desperate but doomed hope that he could retake the state and collect enough reinforcements to confront Union forces in Virginia and the Ohio Valley.

Despite his loss at Franklin, Hood marched his ragtag troops (a quarter of whom didn't even have a pair of shoes to call their own) on to Nashville, where Union forces, under the command of George Thomas, awaited. The ensuing battle was devastating to the Confederates. Thomas's army, combined with that of John Schofield, fresh from Franklin, was nearly twice the size of Hood's. Worse, federal forces had occupied Nashville since early 1862 and had fortified the city to the point where it was nearly impenetrable.

Hood and his army arrived in the hills south of Nashville on December 2 and found themselves in a serious quandary. They lacked the manpower and weapons to attack or lay siege, and they couldn't go around the city without exposing their rear flank. So Hood did the only thing he could do: He formed a defensive line and waited for Thomas to attack, hoping and praying that reinforcements would arrive before the inevitable battle started.

On the morning of December 15, three Union corps smashed the Confederate left while supplemental infantry and cavalry drew the attention of Confederate troops at the other end of the defensive line. Hood's army fought as best it could against overwhelming numbers but finally was forced to fall back to a new position between two hills about two miles away.

In the darkness, Thomas couldn't tell if Hood's army had merely pulled back or had actually retreated, so he waited until the following afternoon to renew his attack. Hood's men managed to successfully push back a charge on Overton Hill, but by 4 P.M. Hood's entire left flank was surrounded by Union infantry and artillery. As a hard rain began to fall, the Union troops managed to smash through the Confederate line with frightening force, routing the panic-stricken rebels. Nearly an entire division, including its artillery, was captured in the fray, along with a large amount of other supplies. The remaining soldiers of the Army of Tennessee found themselves pursued by Union horsemen after the rout. They ran for nearly two weeks, covered in the rear by Nathan Bedford Forrest's cavalry, until they reached Mississippi.

The Battle of Nashville was a resounding success for the Union and was won with relatively light casualties—about 400 Union soldiers killed and approximately 1,500 Confederates killed or wounded. Hood resigned his command in January, and his remaining troops were reassigned to the eastern theater, where they were give the hopeless task of stopping Sherman's march through the Carolinas.

49.
CAT AND MOUSE
IN PETERSBURG

JUNE 15, 1864–APRIL 3, 1865. Grant and Lee spent the final months of the war in a deadly game of cat and mouse. Grant outmanned and outgunned his Confederate counterpart, but he never seemed able to get Lee's army into a position in which it could be destroyed once and for all. The fighting culminated in the Siege of Petersburg, a 10-month standoff that ended only after the Confederate army, worn down by almost non-stop fighting, could no longer defend itself against a frontal assault.

Lee had handed Grant a humiliating defeat at the Battle of Cold Harbor, Virginia, on June 3, 1864, and nine days later, much to Lee's bewilderment, Grant quietly began moving his Army of the Potomac. His destination was Petersburg, a town about 20 miles south of Richmond that was vital to the Confederate capital's railway supply lines and communications. Grant knew that if he could take Petersburg, Richmond would not be far behind.

A 2,100-foot pontoon bridge was quickly built by army engineers so that Union troops could cross the James River and, on June 15, an advance guard of more than 10,000 men commanded by William F. Smith stood ready to descend on Petersburg. The city was defended by a tiny Confederate army of just 2,500 men, led by Pierre G. T. Beauregard, but Smith didn't know that. Assuming the opposing army to be much larger, he proceeded with extraordinary caution, coming close to taking the city. However, Beauregard's soldiers managed to hold off the Union assault just long enough for Lee and the Army of Northern Virginia to come to their rescue.

Grant's hopes for a quick victory in Petersburg (and a quick end to the war itself) were destroyed. Having no other recourse, he laid siege on the city, bombarding it daily with heavy artillery in the hope that he could drive Lee to surrender. Lee, meanwhile, grew increasingly frustrated. He knew that his army was greatly outnumbered and that his stand at Petersburg in defense of Richmond was a losing cause. He could hold out for a while, but not forever.

Grant tried to hasten the situation by extending his offensive line, a complicated maze of trenches, more than 40 miles around to the southwest of Petersburg. Lee was forced to follow suit, stretching his defenses to the very limit. Despite the hardships in the trenches, Lee's fortifications were incredibly solid and successfully repelled repeated Union assaults.

As the siege continued, Union forces slowly and methodically increased their stranglehold on the enemy by severing vital supply lines. Lee realized that he had little chance of successfully holding off Grant's growing army and formed a plan that involved leaving the trenches around Petersburg and joining forces with Joseph E. Johnston's army in North Carolina. On March 25, John Gordon attacked the Union line east of the city in a desperate attempt to carve out a path by which Lee's army could escape. The rebel forces managed to capture Fort Stedman and nearly a half-mile of Union trenches, but they were finally forced back by a Union counterattack.

Grant extended his offensive line several miles to the west in an attempt to break Lee's already weakened defenses. On April 1, infantry and cavalry from both sides met at Five Forks Junction, and after a heated battle, George Pickett's Confederate division was broken and routed. That opened the door for Grant's final attack. At 4:30 A.M. on April 2, Union forces started a massive assault along the entire Confederate defensive line. The horribly outnumbered Confederate troops couldn't hold off the onslaught, and Union troops broke through at several places. Petersburg had fallen.

Lee had no recourse but to retreat. He sent word to Jefferson Davis that Petersburg would soon be in Union hands and that Richmond should be evacuated immediately, then headed west along the Appomattox River in search of food and some way to join Johnston's army. Grant, unwilling to let Lee's troops escape and regroup yet again, followed close behind. The two commanders skirmished for several more days, but Lee quickly realized there was no way he could win against Grant's much larger army. On April 9, the two men met in the home of Wilmer McLean in Appomattox Court House to discuss terms of surrender.

50.
WARFARE ON THE WATER

THOUGH MOST OF THE MAJOR battles in the Civil War occurred on land, naval warfare also played an integral role in the conflict's final outcome, especially in the western theater. The navies on both sides developed startling new innovations, such as the ironclad ship and the submarine, and changed forever the way sea battles would be fought.

The first naval involvement was a blockade of Southern ports ordered by President Lincoln just a few days after the attack on Fort Sumter. Lincoln believed a blockade would strangle the new republic's ability to do business with foreign powers and thus force it toward a quick peace. But while

Lincoln's intentions may have been good, the U.S. Navy's ability to carry out the plan was not.

At the onset of the war, the U.S. Navy's fleet was in shambles. It had only 90 ships, and most of them were obsolete. In fact, when Lincoln first called for a blockade, only three ships were available for immediate duty— three ships to cover more than 3,500 miles of Southern coastline. In addition, the majority of Union navy personnel were spread across the world and unavailable for immediate service (and of those that were, nearly 10 percent resigned their commission to join the Confederacy). As a result, Confederate blockade runners, which were typically painted gray to avoid detection, came and went with impunity for the first couple of years of the war.

The Union blockade became more effective as the war progressed. In 1861, at the beginning of the war, only one in ten blockade runners was captured. By 1864, that number had risen to one in three. A number of different types of blockades were used. Some Southern ports were close-blockaded and attacked by a combination of army and navy forces. Out at sea, a cruising blockade was often established in international waters, along well-traveled sea lanes and in neutral ports.

The Union navy may have been less than adequate at the onset of the war, but even with its many faults, it was still superior to the Confederate navy. Stephen Mallory, Confederate secretary of the navy, described the

Conflict of Interest   **Not surprisingly, the Confederate government balked at cruising blockades, calling them a violation of international law. But the Union found them effective.**

Confederate navy in 1861 as consisting only of an unfurnished room, in which naval policy was formed, in Montgomery, Alabama. However, under Mallory, the Confederate navy quickly made up for its deficiencies and soon proved a viable threat to the Union war effort. It's estimated that one-sixth of Confederate naval officers came from the North at the beginning of the war, among them navigator Matthew Fontaine Maury and Franklin Buchanan, former commandant of the Washington Navy Yard.

The Confederate naval forces consisted primarily of two types: commerce destroyers (modeled after the pirate-like privateers that preyed on British merchant ships during the Revolutionary War and the War of 1812) and ironclad ships that were used almost exclusively to protect rivers and harbors.

51.
FARRAGUT SAILS INTO NEW ORLEANS

APRIL 25, 1862. David Farragut's bold attack on New Orleans placed the city and its port under Union command, a striking defeat for the Confederacy. By taking New Orleans, located 100 miles above the mouth of the Mississippi River, the Union effectively controlled the very gateway to the Deep South.

New Orleans was an important Confederate city, vital to trade and commerce. However, military actions in other regions left it only lightly defended. Its greatest protection from Union invasion came from Fort Jackson and Fort St. Philip, which guarded the water approach 75 miles down river.

Naval Commander David Porter believed that a strong mortar attack from boats on the river could disable the forts' firepower and allow a fleet to pass all the way to New Orleans; such an attack was readied in the early months of 1862.

To facilitate the invasion, Union General Benjamin Butler captured Ship Island, near the mouth of the Mississippi. Here, Squadron Captain David Farragut (Porter's adopted brother) assembled a fleet of 24 wooden sloops and gunboats, which were combined with Porter's 19 mortar schooners. The ships were renovated to make them lighter so that they could pass over the river's many sandbars, and the fleet began its long trip up the Mississippi in April 1862, supported by Butler's 15,000 troops for a possible land invasion.

On April 18, Porter put his plan into action, slamming the two forts with a six-day mortar attack. His 19 mortar ships lobbed more than 3,000 shells at the forts each day, but aside from making a horrible racket, they did little damage to the forts' defenses. The bombardment did act as a distraction, however, and on the night of April 20, two Union gunboats approached the river barricade and cleared a small path for the rest of the fleet.

When it became evident that mortars were not having much of an impact, Farragut ordered his fleet to proceed past them anyway, hopeful that enough ships would survive the gauntlet to invade the city of New Orleans. The fleet began the treacherous run under the cover of darkness early on the morning of April 24 and was quickly met with cannon fire. The mortar ships responded in kind, and the artillery duel lit up the sky over the Mississippi as if it were a July 4 fireworks display. In addition, Confederate officers tried to halt the invasion by sending out a small fleet of wooden ships to ram the approaching Union vessels. Several rafts that had been set on fire were also deployed in an attempt to slow the advance.

All but four of Farragut's fleet made it safely past the supposedly unpassable Confederate forts. Approximately 170 men were killed or injured during the assault.

Farragut sailed into New Orleans on April 25 and captured the city with little resistance, though the mayor of the city refused to officially surrender. The soldiers manning Forts Jackson and St. Philip laid down their guns on April 28, and Butler and his troops arrived the next day, quickly occupying the city of New Orleans despite a belligerent and antagonistic populace.

52.
NAVAL
SHOWDOWN
IN MEMPHIS

JUNE 6, 1862. After a solid victory at Corinth, the Union army turned its attention to Memphis, Tennessee, the Confederacy's fifth largest city and a key port. But before Henry Halleck had a chance to invade, the city fell during one of the war's most impressive naval engagements.

In order to reach Memphis, Union forces had to take Island No. 10 and Fort Pillow, which stood just 50 miles above Memphis. The fort was armed with 40 guns, and Confederates had hedged their bet with a fleet of eight steamboats that had been converted into armed rams, a throwback to the days of the Roman galley. These rams surprised the Union fleet with a hit-and-run attack at Plum Run Bend, located just above Fort Pillow, and disabled two Union ironclads by punching holes in them just below the waterline.

Ellet was eager to take on the Confederate fleet at Fort Pillow, but his plans changed when Beauregard ordered the evacuation of Fort Pillow after his withdrawal from Corinth. Instead, the Confederates decided to make a stand at Memphis, and early on June 6, the Southern ram fleet sailed out to take on five Union ironclads and four of Ellet's self-designed ram ships.

Sign of the Changing Times   The Union navy vowed never to be caught unprepared again and fitted several steamboats of its own with sturdy rams. The brains behind the operation was Charles Ellet, a 57-year-old civil engineer from Pennsylvania who, having failed to convince the Union navy of the value of ram power, found a believer in Secretary of War Stanton.

Thousands of Memphis residents lined the bluffs above the river to cheer the rebels.

When the smoke cleared, they had taken out two crippled Confederate boats, sank another, and captured three others after they had been disabled. Only one Confederate boat escaped the battle. It was a devastating defeat for the Confederate river force and opened the door for the Union capture of Memphis. The residents who had so loudly cheered their side during the early minutes of the river battle stood silent as a four-man detachment led by Ellet's son, Charles junior, raised the American flag over the Memphis post office. Charles senior was wounded in the fighting and died two weeks later. Charles junior was promoted to colonel—at 19, the youngest person to hold that rank—and took command of his father's ram fleet. He was killed a year later in combat.

53.
THE BATTLE OF MOBILE BAY, "DAMN THE TORPEDOES, FULL SPEED AHEAD"

AUGUST 5, 1864. Alabama's Mobile Bay became increasingly important to the Confederacy as the war progressed. The Union blockade had effectively closed other ports, but Mobile Bay was still relatively free, making it the only open gulf port east of Texas and the primary site for the smuggling of arms and provisions from Europe. U.S. Navy Rear Admiral David Farragut wanted to launch an assault on the port immediately following his success at New Orleans in April 1862, but circumstances forced him to wait until January 1864 to begin preparations. The attack itself wouldn't come for another seven months.

When the time came, however, Farragut had an impressive fleet behind him: 14 wooden boats and four ironclads. He began the assault early on the morning of August 5, easing the fleet into the bay, which was heavily mined with what were known back than as torpedoes. The fleet was met by heavy Confederate gunfire from Fort Morgan, the bay's main defense, as well as a Confederate fleet of three wooden gunboats and the South's largest ironclad, the *CSS Tennessee*, led by Confederate Admiral Franklin Buchanan.

As the battle commenced, Farragut tied himself high in the rigging of his flagship, the *Hartford*, so that he could better direct his ships. From his perch, he watched his lead ironclad, the *Tecumseh* strike a mine and sink with almost all hands in a matter of minutes. The rest of Farragut's ships stopped where they were, confused and fearful of other mines, as the cannons at Fort Morgan continued to roar. It was then that Farragut shouted the rallying words for which he is still remembered today: "Damn the torpedoes! Full speed ahead!" Moving the *Hartford* out in front, Farragut successfully led his fleet through the minefield and past the fort into Mobile Bay.

The *Tennessee*, commanded by Buchanan himself, tried to ram the Union ships, then engaged in a gun battle with them before slinking off to safe harbor at Fort Morgan. The Union crews took that quiet moment to have a quick breakfast, only to have their meal interrupted by the *Tennessee*, which had returned for another attack. The Confederate ironclad was a formidable ship, but Buchanan soon found himself surrounded by Union vessels, which rammed and fired upon his ship until it was a helpless hulk. Buchanan was injured during the battle and his ship surrendered at around 10. A.M. In just four hours, Mobile Bay had come under Union control. Fort Morgan, however, was not captured until August 23, and the city of Mobile would remain in Confederate hands until the following April.

54
THE *MONITOR* VS.
THE *MERRIMACK*

MARCH 19, 1862. One of the best-known naval battles during the Civil War was the duel between the Union ironclad *Monitor* and the Confederate ironclad *Virginia*, formerly the USS *Merrimac*.

The Confederacy dredged up the *Merrimac*, which had been torched and scuttled by Union forces when the Confederacy took control of the Norfolk shipyards, and turned it into the first ironclad vessel to be built on American soil. News of the venture quickly reached Union officials, who immediately approved the development of ironclads for the Union navy. The first to be constructed (in a remarkable 101 days) was the *Monitor*. Like the *Virginia*, the *Monitor* was protected by 4-inch steel plates. However, it had two guns on a revolving turret, which provided more accurate firepower. It also was smaller, faster, and more maneuverable than the *Virginia*.

The *Virginia* sailed into Chesapeake Bay on March 5 and headed for Hampton Roads, a major Union blockading base. On March 8, at around 1 P.M., the ship confronted five wooden Union ships, which didn't know what to make of the bizarre vessel facing them. They fired all they had at the partially submerged craft but quickly found that their shells had little impact aside from making a horrific noise. The *Virginia* immediately set about its task, ramming and sinking the *Cumberland*, one of the Union's most impressive frigates, grounding and burning the 50-gun *Congress*; and knocking out of commission the flagship *Minnesota*. The only damage to the ironclad was a broken ram and injuries to its captain, Franklin Buchanan.

To the rescue sailed the USS *Monitor*, though it almost didn't make it. The ship nearly sank as it ponderously sailed to Hampton Roads, arriving around 1 A.M. on March 9. Officials in Washington feared that the Union ironclad would be no match for the *Virginia* but the *Monitor* soon proved otherwise. The two ships faced off, just 100 yards apart, at 9 A.M. on March 9 and began pounding each other. Shells bounced off their iron skins, and the two ships collided several times, sometimes by accident and sometimes not. The furious duel lasted four hours, with neither side gaining an advantage. The *Monitor* finally drew back when its captain, John L. Worden, was temporarily blinded by a shell blast, and the *Virginia*, which was slowly taking on water and experiencing engine difficulties, took that as its cue to withdraw. The battle ended in a draw, though it could be said that the Union was the real victor because its blockade of Hampton Roads survived. The battle of the ironclads foreshadowed an end of wooden war ships and a shift to iron and eventually steel in shipbuilding.

PART THREE

THE WEAPONS OF WAR

AS BOTH SIDES SCRAMBLED TO PUT TOGETHER A fighting force, Union ordnance officials weren't too concerned about the state of the nation's arsenals. Secretary of War Simon Cameron and Chief of Ordnance James Ripley both believed that the number of guns readily available for service, though small, would be sufficient for a war everyone thought would last three months at best. After all, the number of troops necessary to bring the Southern rebellion under control was estimated at 250,000, and the federal weapons stores housed more than 400,000 rifles and muskets, which would also be supplemented with weapons brought by state militias.

However, the picture of the war changed dramatically after the first few battles, which demonstrated that the South was not going down without a long and costly fight. Not surprisingly, the Union's entire supply of modern rifled weapons, which included 40,000 Model 1855 Harpers Ferry rifles, rifle muskets, and other weapons, were disbursed during the first six weeks of the war.

55.
THE THINGS
THEY CARRIED

SMALL ARMS ARE ANY WEAPONS smaller than a cannon and carried by a soldier. During the Civil War, the most common small arms included the following:

- **Muskets**—smoothbore, long-barreled shoulder arms

- **Rifles**—shoulder arms with spiral grooves cut into the inner surface of the barrel

- **Carbines**—short-barreled rifles, commonly used by the cavalry

- **Handguns**—pistols and revolvers

Small arms were commonly designated by their caliber, method of loading (breech or muzzle), and manufacturer. The most frequently used small arms in both the Union and Confederate armies were the .58 caliber Springfield musket and the .69 caliber Harpers Ferry rifle. Both were muzzle-loaded weapons that fired the Minie ball, a revolutionary hollow-based bullet that greatly accelerated the loading and firing process.

The increased use of these weapons resulted in a remarkable change in infantry tactics. Smoothbore muskets were notoriously inaccurate and had a relatively short range; firing lines as close as 100 yards inflicted little damage. For maximum effectiveness, soldiers usually had to run toward the enemy firing en masse and hope they hit something, then use their bayonets for close-quarter fighting. The rifled musket introduced just prior to the Civil War was a completely different weapon, however. It offered accuracy at a considerable distance (skilled snipers could hit their target as far as a half mile away), which made a frontal assault especially hazardous. Unfortunately, many commanding officers failed to take these new weapons into consideration when formulating battle strategy, resulting in a huge number of casualties.

56.
MUSKETS
AND RIFLES

THE PICTURE OF THE WAR changed dramatically after the first few battles, which demonstrated that the South was not going down without a long and costly fight. Not surprisingly, the Union's entire supply of modern rifled weapons, which included 40,000 Model 1855 Harpers Ferry rifles, rifle muskets, and other weapons, were disbursed during the first six weeks of the war.

It wasn't until mid-1861 that the federal armory in Springfield, Massachusetts, started producing what would become the favored weapon during the war—the Model 1861 Springfield rifle musket. Before that, the average Union soldier had to make due with the traditional smooth-bore musket, a weapon with a high-risk factor because of its inaccuracy and time-consuming loading procedure. Demand for the Model 1861 was tremendous.

Some of the most impressive weapons in the federal arsenal were the .58-caliber rifled arms, most of them altered Mississippis and U.S. Model 1855s. Manufactured to conform to the new standards for arms established

On the Homefront **The Springfield Armory produced more than 250,000 of the weapons over two years, and the government still had to contract with 20 private manufacturers to make an additional 450,000. Each cost the U.S. Treasury between $15 and $20.**

by Jefferson Davis, who was then secretary of war, in July 1855, the guns were designed to fire the .58-caliber Minie ball, which was easier to load and offered greater accuracy. The elimination of all calibers but the .58 from its muzzleloading regulation arms helped the government simplify weapons production.

Weapons were also obtained from foreign manufacturers. In April 1861, for example, Captain Caleb Huse was sent to Europe by Confederate officials to purchase as many small arms as he possibly could. The result was a wide array of weapons that varied greatly in quality. British Enfield rifle muskets were greatly coveted by Confederate infantry, but others, such as the Austrian Lorenz rifle musket, proved to be shoddily made and fairly ineffectual in the battlefield.

57.
HANDGUNS

ACCORDING TO GOVERNMENT REPORTS, the Union purchased just over 370,000 handguns over the course of the Civil War. The most preferred were the Colt and Remington .44 caliber (known as the Army) and .36 caliber (known as the Navy) six-shooters. They were well-made, reliable, and accurate weapons that packed a punch. A small number of foreign-made handguns were also purchased by Union ordnance officials, such as the Lefaucheux .41-caliber revolver, which was unique in that it was a non-percussion firearm that required a self-exploding pin-fire cartridge. The U.S. government bought about 12,000 Lefaucheux revolvers, most of which were used by soldiers in the western theater.

Because the government doled out handguns only to cavalrymen and mounted light artillery, the number of government-purchased sidearms was greatly exceeded by the number purchased privately by individual soldiers. A good sidearm set back the average soldier about $20, and at the beginning of the war, every well-armed soldier had a handgun on his person to complement his shoulder arm. (Favored handguns included the Colt

Model 1862 police revolver and the Smith and Wesson No. 2 army revolver.) However, as the war progressed, most soldiers found sidearms to be of little use (just as Major Leonidas Scranton noted) and to add unwanted weight. As a result, a great many sidearms were given away, sold, sent home, or merely tossed aside by Union soldiers, who found them more trouble than they were worth.

Confederate soldiers also found sidearms to be a real encumbrance on the battlefield, though Southern cavalrymen preferred them during the close quarters of a full cavalry attack because they were lightweight and extremely accurate at short range. But as with many other things, the South simply couldn't make or acquire enough of them to meet the demand, so one Confederate ordnance officer presented a simple solution to Secretary of War Benjamin: Take the handguns away from the infantry and give them to the cavalry, which needed them more. Benjamin agreed.

The handguns that were used to arm Confederate soldiers came from a multitude of sources, including Southern manufacturers, seized arsenals, fallen soldiers in the battlefield, foreign manufacturers, and private donations from Confederate citizens. Weapons of choice include the Colt "Army" revolver, the Colt "Navy" revolver, and the British-produced Adams and Deane revolver, a double-action .44-caliber sidearm greatly preferred by Confederate officers. The Adams and Deane and the Kerr revolvers were manufactured by the London Armoury Company, the largest single producer of handguns imported into the South. Over the course of the war, thousands of guns were purchased from the company, which was renowned for its quality craftsmanship, and smuggled past the Northern blockade.

58.
SWORDS AND SABERS

SWORDS AND SABERS ARE TRADITIONAL WEAPONS of war and were an important part of every officer's dress uniform on both sides of the Civil War. Among the enlisted men in the Union army, however, only sergeants, cavalry members, select artillerymen, and musicians were issued swords, and rather plain ones at that, since they were designed more for fighting than dress. The swords issued to officers tended to be much more ornate and served as a symbol of rank rather than a fighting weapon. Only the sabers carried by cavalry and light artillery officers were actual weapons, though they weren't used as often as rifles and sidearms.

The vast majority of regulation swords issued to Union soldiers were patterned on weapons of the French army and most were made by private firms or purchased from foreign manufacturers. European sword makers provided nearly all officers' blades, which were based on an 1850 pattern. It was also common for citizens and military subordinates to give specially made presentation swords to officers as tokens of appreciation for exceptional service or bravery, or as a symbol of esteem. Most of these very ornate swords, which were quite expensive, were for formal occasions rather than actual fighting.

Swords held much greater appeal among Confederate soldiers because they harkened back to an era of chivalry and romance, an era that was still in effect in the mid-century South. As in the North, swords were both a symbol of rank and a fighting weapon, though rarely used. Instead, cavalry and artillery forces came to rely on sidearms for self-defense because they were reliable and effective.

Most Confederate swords were variations of models used by the U.S. Army and were manufactured by Southern companies. A large number of Confederate officers, however, wore imported swords, cherished family heirlooms, or U.S. swords acquired during service in the prewar army.

In addition to their sidearms, many Confederate soldiers carried large bowie knives, named after James Bowie, one of the heroes of the Alamo, who was said to have originated the knife's design. The knives were large—blades ranged from 6 to 18 inches in length—and served a number of functions, including skinning wild animals, scaling fish, whittling branches, and self-defense. During man-to-man fighting, a well-honed bowie knife could take off a man's arm with a single swipe.

Sign of the Changing Times   **Confederate infantry officers commonly wore swords but used them in combat only when absolutely necessary.**

59.
ARTILLERY FIRE

ALL FIREARMS LARGER THAN SMALL ARMS are known collectively as artillery or cannon. Several dozen different types of artillery were used over the course of the Civil War, but they all fell into one of two distinct categories: smoothbore or rifled cannon. Artillery was further identified by the weight of their projectile, the caliber of their bore diameter, their method of loading (muzzle or breech), and sometimes the name of their inventor or manufacturer.

The most commonly used artillery on both sides was the Napoleon, a smoothbore, muzzleloaded, 12-pound howitzer. It was developed in France during the reign of Louis Napoleon and was first introduced in the United States in 1856. The Napoleon was a reliable, sturdy piece of machinery that worked equally well as an offensive and defensive weapon.

Second to the Napoleon were the 3-inch ordnance and Parrott guns, rifled cannon that had greater accuracy and range than smoothbore artillery. On a good day, a 3-incher could lob a shell up to 2,500 yards, but such long-range artillery proved ineffective during most battles because the gunner had to see what he was shooting at. Rifled cannon did have their valuable uses, however. They were very good at destroying fortifications and played an integral role in the battles of Vicksburg and Atlanta. Most of the artillery used during the Civil War was muzzleloaded. Breechloading cannons were available, but most gunners found them unreliable and difficult to use.

Size played an important role in the use of artillery; the heavier guns were more difficult to transport, especially over hilly or muddy terrain. The most portable artillery and thus some of the most widely used were the 6- and 12-pound mountain howitzers, which proved very effective during battles fought in the mountainous western theater. Naval and siege cannons were some of the heaviest and provided the greatest power. The 8- and 10-inch siege howitzers had ranges of more than 2,000 yards and could fire 45- and 90-pound shells, which inflicted tremendous damage on their targets.

60.
THE IRONCLADS

ONE OF THE MOST DRAMATIC innovations in naval warfare was the ironclad ship, another Civil War first. These floating fortresses were almost impregnable and changed the face of ocean warfare forever.

At the beginning of the war, iron-armored vessels were still being tentatively explored. The British navy had two ironclad ships and the French had one, and that was all in the entire world. But that would change quickly as the Civil War progressed. Within a year, both sides were ravaging the wooden ships of the other with "floating tin cans" that, while unwieldy, proved to be extremely formidable vessels. Interestingly, it was the Confederate navy that first decided to give the new technology a try. The Union navy was confident its armada of heavily armed wooden ships would be sufficient and didn't follow suit until it became evident that it had no choice.

The idea of putting iron plating on a ship made tremendous sense, so much so that it's surprising it wasn't done earlier. Even iron plating a few inches thick provided sufficient protection from the most commonly used

On the Homefront One of the very first ironclad vessels manufactured on American soil was the *Manassas*, a Confederate prototype that was said to look like a turtle. The Confederates quickly realized the tremendous value of ironclad ships and set about manufacturing as many of them as they could.

artillery shells, and no one at that time had invented an armor-piercing shell. With good reason, ironclads became the scourge of the waterways.

The first Confederate ironclad was the *Virginia*, and its origins are fascinating. Before it was the *Virginia*, the ship was known as the *Merrimac*, a federal steam frigate. The ship's engines were in bad condition, and the ship was in drydock at the Norfolk Navy Yard when the war started. The navy yard quickly fell under Confederate control, and one of the last things the fleeing Union workers did was set fire to the *Merrimac* and scuttle her. However, Confederate engineers quickly raised the vessel and found it in fairly good shape; only the upper portion of the ship had been severely damaged by fire. This ship, they decided, would become the first serviceable ironclad.

The *Merrimac*, rechristened the *CSS Virginia*, was one of the strangest looking vessels ever to be placed in the water. It floated awkwardly, sailed slowly, and was extremely difficult to steer, but it was also unbeatable. No wooden ship could touch it. Shots from naval cannons simply bounced off its metal shell, doing no more damage than a small dent. The Confederates had created the ultimate naval weapon.

The Union quickly learned of the Confederate plans to turn the scuttled *Merrimac* into an ironclad vessel, and in August 1861, the U.S. Congress authorized the development of ironclads for the Union navy. The first Union iron-clad was the *USS Monitor*, which engaged in a two-hour duel with the *CSS Virginia* in Chesapeake Bay on March 9, 1862. It ended in a draw, but with that single engagement, the era of the wooden naval vessel came to an end.

61.
NON-UNIFORM
UNIFORMS

THE CIVIL WAR IS COMMONLY known as the War of the Blue and the Gray, describing the colors of the uniforms worn by Union and Confederate soldiers. But in truth, there was very little conformity of dress on either side, at least during the first months of the war. The regular army had an established uniform, but the majority of participants were volunteers from state militias who often demonstrated their independence and esprit de corps by dressing in flamboyant (albeit impractical) uniforms of their own design. When these units got together, it looked more like a circus show than a fighting force.

The various units fighting for the Confederacy were even more independent in their attire, showing their disdain for the concept of a centralized government by dressing as colorfully and uniquely as they could. Again, when several different units gathered together, it looked like anything but an army going to war. Only later in the conflict would both sides establish a standard for military dress, though many units tenaciously continued to flaunt their independence by adding flourishes and various accouterments.

One of the biggest problems during the first months of the war was finding enough uniforms to dress the participants on both sides. In the North, a great many clothing manufacturers received lucrative government contracts to make military uniforms, but in the rush to meet quotas, factory-made uniforms were often of poor quality and design. The system also fostered corruption, which only made the situation worse. Eventually, the government cracked down on manufacturers who churned out inferior clothing while pocketing huge profits, and the quality of uniforms improved dramatically.

The U.S. Quartermaster Department was responsible for dressing the Union's fighting forces, having supervised the design and manufacture of clothing for enlisted men at the Schuylkill Arsenal since the War of 1812.

But the states were also unable to supply adequate numbers of uniforms on such short notice, so many early volunteer regiments wore uniforms paid for by their local communities, with perhaps a little help from the state.

On the Homefront **However, the army was hard pressed to adequately dress the huge influx of new soldiers at the beginning of the war, so the War Department asked the various states to dress their own regiments—preferably in the traditional dark blue uniform—and apply to the government for reimbursement.**

As odd as it may seem today, several regiments left for Washington without any uniforms at all. The 1st and 2d Ohio, for example, were sent to the nation's capital so soon after they were organized that their leaders decided to pick up uniforms during the trip rather than wait. However, their agent found the market in Pennsylvania overwhelmed by state purchasers, so he bought whole material instead and had the uniforms made by Pennsylvania tailors. The resulting uniforms could only be described as casual. In fact, some didn't even have buttons! But these problems were quickly remedied, and the regiments marched into Washington looking almost like real soldiers.

62.
SOLDIER'S
CLOTHES

EXOTIC UNIFORMS ASIDE, THE typical Union infantryman wore a dark blue, loose flannel sackcoat that hung at mid-thigh; blue trousers made of wool or jersey; a light blouse; heavy leather shoes that were derisively known as "gunboats"; and a blue forage cap, also known as a slouch cap. Additional clothing and protective gear included an overcoat with a blue cape; a thick wool blanket (which weighed approximately five pounds);

a gum blanket that served as a tent floor (as well as a poncho, during inclement weather); a thick flannel pullover shirt, and a pair of wool socks.

Affiliation with a specific branch of the service was indicated by stripes down the outer seam of the uniform—yellow for cavalry, red for artillery, light blue for infantry, emerald green for mounted rifleman, and crimson for ordnance and hospital personnel. Distinctions in rank were denoted by the type of frock coat worn—majors, lieutenant colonels, colonels, and all general officers wore double-breasted coats; lower ranking officers wore single-breasted coats.

Noncommissioned officers wore a single row of nine buttons. Sergeants wore three chevrons on their sleeves, and corporals wore two chevrons. Regular troops wore one stripe sewn on the lower sleeves for every five years of service.

The uniforms worn by Confederate troops were quite similar to their Union counterparts, except the color was gray or yellow-brown. The standard infantryman wore a gray or yellow-brown wool shell jacket; gray, yellow-brown, or blue pants; low-heeled leather shoes; and a gray or yellow-brown forage cap. Frock coats similar to those worn by Union infantry were also part of the uniform, but supplies were limited, and not all soldiers received them. Additional garments traditionally included a homemade coverlet, a cotton shirt, a wool vest, and wool socks. All officers and enlisted men on both sides also received ankle-high boots.

In the Confederate army, affiliation with a particular branch of service for artillery, light blue for infantry, and black for medical personnel. Variations in rank within each branch was designated by colored stripes on outer trouser seams—regimental officers had a ¼-inch stripe; generals wore a 2⅝-inch stripe; adjutant, quartermaster, commissary, and engineer officers wore one gold ¼-inch stripe. Noncommissioned officers wore a ¼-inch cotton stripe of colors appropriate to their branch of service.

Rank was also indicated by buttons and insignias. Generals, lieutenant generals, major generals, and brigadier generals wore three gold stars (the middle one larger than the other two) within a wreath on their collars. Colonels wore three stars of equal size, lieutenant colonels wore two stars, and majors wore one star. Captains and first lieutenants wore two gold bars, and second lieutenants wore one bar. Sergeants wore three chevrons on their sleeves, and corporals wore two chevrons. A brigadier general's coat had two rows of eight buttons, and a junior officer's coat had two rows of seven buttons each.

Soldiers on both sides were expected to carry all of their provisions, including clothing, equipment, personal effects, and weapons, on their backs, and a fully equipped infantryman might carry a load of 50 pounds or more. On long marches, the burden could be quite heavy.

63.
FLAGS OF THE NORTH AND SOUTH

THE NATIONAL FLAGS OF the Union and the Confederacy were more than colorful pieces of cloth; they quickly came to symbolize everything each side stood for, rallying troops and private citizens into a patriotic fervor unlike anything that had ever been seen before. In New York City, for example, an angry mob took over the offices of the New York Herald, which held a strong pro-Southern sentiment, and threatened to burn everything in sight if publisher James Gordon Bennett didn't display the Stars and Stripes. He quickly complied.

Indeed, it became quite fashionable to display the flag at one's home and office, and to wear the flag on one's person as a show of support for the Union cause. And the same was true for the Confederate "Stars and Bars." Failure to revere the flag of one's republic was viewed as extremely unpatriotic. Communities nationwide presented specially made flags—either traditional designs or variations thereof—to local militia units gearing up to go to war, hopeful that the colorful banners would inspire the troops to victory.

In 1861, U.S. Army regulations were revised to require infantry units to carry two silk flags, a national flag and a regimental flag, each nearly six feet square.

The Flags of the Confederacy were different. Prior to the official formation of the Confederacy, many of the seceding states asserted their independence by abandoning the Stars and Stripes and adopting new flags that fell into three distinct categories. States with a strong colonial tradition, such as Virginia and South Carolina, chose symbols—typically a coat of arms—on a blue field. States with less of a colonial attachment, such as Alabama, proclaimed their independence by placing a single star (which represented them on the American flag) on a blue field. And other states chose to symbolize their secession by displaying a single star as the prominent device. Louisiana, for example, adopted a flag that had a field of 13 alternating red, white, and blue stripes, with a single yellow star in its red canton.

64.
MUSIC ON THE
BATTLEFIELD

MUSIC PLAYED AN INTEGRAL ROLE in the Civil War. Bands performed during war rallies, they were used as a recruitment tool, and they helped inspire troops during battle engagements.

The U.S. War Department officially sanctioned regimental brass bands in May 1861. By decree, each infantry or artillery regiment was permitted one 24-man band, and cavalry regiments were allowed a 16-man ensemble. Regimental brass bands were so popular that a U.S. Sanitation Commission inspection of Union military camps in October 1861 found that nearly 75 percent of all regiments had one. Bands were very common within the Confederate army, too, and it wasn't unusual for musicians from both sides to serenade each other across the lines.

When not playing their instruments, band members performed a number of other functions, such as that of medical assistant. At Little Round Top during the Battle of Gettysburg, musicians from the 20th Maine aided surgeons performing fast and furious amputations—the medical procedure of choice on the battlefield. When not actually assisting doctors, band members often played their instruments to cheer up wounded soldiers in field hospitals.

Union and Confederate regiments without actual bands still had musicians, usually fife players or drummers for infantry units and buglers for cavalry units. Most of the daily aspects of camp life, such as reveille, were governed by these musicians, who also helped orchestrate with bugle blasts or drum rolls important tactical movements on the battlefield.

Sadly, the use of large brass bands was short lived within the Union army. In July 1862, the U.S. adjutant general ordered all volunteer regimental brass ensembles disbanded due to the high cost of their maintenance. Some unit leaders managed to keep their bands intact by having the members re-enlist as regular soldiers and then detailing them to serve as musicians. But ultimately, the majority of units were left with just their drum corps to keep them entertained.

PART FOUR

THE HORRORS OF WAR

FOR SOLDIERS, COMBAT DURING THE CIVIL WAR WAS a nightmarish experience, as was everyday life. The average soldier found himself battling a litany of camp problems, ranging from sheer boredom to disease and death. For many soldiers, camp was home for up to three years, travel was by foot, death was a common sight, and being taken prisoner was a daily concern.

65.
CAMP LIFE

ARMY REGULATIONS REQUIRED CAMPS to be laid out in a grid pattern, with officers' quarters at the front end of each street and enlisted men's quarters aligned to the rear. The camp was set up approximately along the same lines as the line of battle, and each company proudly displayed its colors on the outside of its tents. Military regulations also outlined where the mess tents, medical cabins, and other structures should be located, though the rules were often ignored when the terrain or situation made them difficult to follow.

Because soldiers were forced to bivouac in tents out in the open, the conditions at many camps were less than ideal. This was especially true in the Deep South, where wet weather in the spring and summer turned the ground into thick mud for weeks on end, and dry weather in the fall and winter turned it into suffocating dust.

During the summer months, most soldiers slept in canvas tents. At the onset of the war, both sides used what was known as the Sibley tent, named after its inventor, Henry H. Sibley, who eventually rose to the rank of brigadier general in the Confederate army. The Sibley tent was designed to house 12 men comfortably, but a shortage of supplies often increased occupancy to up to 20 men per tent. As might be expected, the conditions within these tents often bordered on the intolerable. Bathing was a rare luxury for soldiers in the field, so the stench within the tents was suffocating during inclement weather when the flaps had to be lowered.

The Union army primarily used the wedge tent, a 6-foot length of canvas draped over a horizontal pole and staked to the ground at the sides, with flaps that closed over each end. The wedge tent also saw use in the South, but when canvas became scarce, many soldiers were forced to make open-air beds by piling leaves or straw between two logs and covering it with a blanket or poncho. During the winter, crude huts were made out of wood, when wood was available.

During down periods, the typical day started at 5 A.M. during the spring and summer months and 6 A.M. during the fall and winter. Soldiers were awakened by reveille, roll call was taken by the first sergeant, and then everyone sat down to breakfast, which usually consisted of biscuits, some kind of cured meat, and coffee. If available, eggs and fruit were added to the menu.

During the rest of the day, soldiers engaged in as many as five drill sessions, during which they learned how to shoot their weapons with accuracy and perform various maneuvers. Drill sessions lasted about two hours each,

Sign of the Changing Times **Overcrowding was alleviated somewhat when the Sibley tent was replaced by smaller, easier to carry tents.**

and most soldiers found them extremely boring and tedious; they wanted to fight, not just practice, though they realized that when fighting actually occurred, the drills could mean the difference between life and death.

66
CHAOS ON THE BATTLEFIELD

ONCE A BATTLE COMMENCED, the scene was usually one of chaos. The noise was deafening as cannons roared and hundreds and sometimes thousands of soldiers fired on each other. Officers would try desperately to rally and guide their troops in the throes of battle, but the smoke and the noise often made the task difficult, if not impossible. In addition, as many as half of the soldiers typically had little knowledge of the terrain, and it wasn't unusual for entire units to get lost.

Every battle was different; the terrain changed, as did the weather, and even the number of men available to fight varied. Officers did the best they could under these ever-changing circumstances, and many of the most skilled officers managed to pull off some spectacular feats even in the face of overwhelming odds.

Different too were the leadership styles of commanding officers. Some were skilled tacticians and strategists, others were exceptionally skilled at leading their men, and a few could do both. Generals tended to stay toward the rear lines during a battle, guiding the action with the aid of subordinates who would carry orders down to unit leaders. But a few reckless generals liked to lead by example and were out in the front of the charge. Sadly, both sides lost a great number of talented leaders as a result.

67.
A LEGENDARY
LOSS

CAUSES OF DEATH DURING the Civil War were many. Bullets and artillery took their share of lives on both sides, but soldiers also died from disease and other factors. In fact, more than twice as many men died from illness than from enemy fire.

The casualty statistics are staggering. According to an in-depth analysis of government records, slightly more than 350,000 Union soldiers died from various causes during the Civil War. The majority of deaths, as noted, were from disease. And nearly 25,000 men died from causes such as suicide,

On the Homefront **To put these figures in perspective, consider that more Americans died during the Civil War than all other American wars combined, from the Revolutionary War to Vietnam, including both World War I and II.**

execution, sunstroke, and accidents. The Union navy lost nearly 5,000 men to illness, accidents, and battle injuries.

Records of Confederate deaths aren't nearly as comprehensive as those of Union casualties due to the destruction of military and government files during and after the war. However, a generally accepted estimate is 150,000 dead of disease and 95,000 killed or mortally wounded in combat. No statistics survive regarding deaths among Confederate naval personnel.

In fact, the Battle of Antietam, on September 17, 1862, resulted in four times the casualties as the landing on Normandy Beach on June 6, 1944.

The high number of battlefield deaths during the Civil War is easy to understand. The weapons used caused massive physical damage when they hit their targets, and outdated battle tactics often put large numbers of soldiers in harm's way. But the number of deaths related to disease requires a little explanation.

The Civil War took place shortly before a number of important advances in human medicine. There were no vaccines for the most common of illnesses, and hygiene was poor, especially in mobile military camps. Young men who had lived their entire lives in relative seclusion in small towns and hamlets simply didn't have immunity to many types of illnesses, and they fell sick from the most innocuous of diseases.

Soldiers weren't the only ones to die during the Civil War. The conflict also took a huge toll on the civilian population, particularly in the South. While the number of Northern citizens who died as a direct result of the war is relatively small, some historians estimate that up to 50,000 Confederate citizens may have perished from various causes, including stray bullets from battles fought literally in their backyards and poor sanitation following the devastation of entire towns and cities.

68.
PRISONER
EXCHANGE RATE

FOR THE MOST PART, soldiers taken prisoner by both sides were relatively well treated. This was the Victorian era, after all, and chivalry still had its place during wartime. More importantly, however, the soldiers of the North and South weren't fighting some unknown, foreign enemy; they were fighting their own countrymen. To abuse another American, even a rebellious one, wasn't in the nature of most men (though, as with everything, there were exceptions). In addition, every soldier knew that there was a strong possibility he could be taken prisoner, so it behooved all to act with kindness toward captured enemy forces—today it was them; tomorrow it could be you.

At the beginning of the war, captured soldiers were expected to "give parole," or promise not to escape. If parole were offered and accepted, soldiers could expect to be sent back to their own lines under a flag of truce, at which time they would be sent home until an exchange was effected. (Union and Confederate military officials reached an agreement in 1862 that stipulated that all prisoners were to be exchanged within 10 days of capture.) After an official prisoner exchange, paroled soldiers could return to active duty.

The value of a prisoner depended on his rank. During prisoner exchanges, a general was worth up to 60 privates, a major general was worth up to 40 privates, and so forth. At the bottom end, a noncommissioned officer was worth two privates, and privates were traded one for one. Approximately 200,000 soldiers from both sides were freed through prisoner exchanges.

The concept of prisoner parole dates back many years. However, it was followed less and less as the Civil War progressed. In 1864, the Union ceased prisoner exchanges all together in an attempt to bring the Confederacy down by attrition. Prisoner exchanges did nothing but bolster an army's ability to fight, and Union officials finally realized that every Confederate soldier in a POW camp was one less rifle aimed at Union soldiers. The policy had a devastating effect on the South, where manpower shortages were rampant. Unfortunately, many POWs also suffered greatly as a result of the no-exchange policy.

The conditions at POW camps varied greatly. At the beginning of the war, when prisoner exchanges helped keep prisons relatively empty, conditions were fairly good on both sides. Prisoners were usually well treated, well fed, and adequately clothed. This remained true for most prisons in the North throughout the war, but the conditions of POW camps in the South deteriorated greatly as the Confederacy gradually found itself unable to feed and clothe even its own citizens and soldiers. The Georgia prison known as Andersonville is probably best known for the squalid and barbaric conditions in which Northern prisoners were housed, but it wasn't alone. Most prison officials did their best to maintain humane conditions, but they had less and less to work with during the final year of the war.

69.
ANDERSONVILLE
HORROR

NO PRISONER OF WAR camp was more reviled than the Confederate prison constructed near the village of Andersonville in Sumter County, Georgia. Its name has become synonymous with barbarism and ill treatment.

Andersonville was opened in February 1864, after the high number of Northern prisoners started taking a heavy toll on the food supplies in Richmond, where prisoners had previously been housed. When the first prisoners arrived at the new camp, they were greeted by 16 acres of open land surrounded by a 15-foot-tall stockade. Originally designed to house 10,000 men, the facility soon contained more than three times that number and was expanded to 26 acres. Nearly 400 new prisoners arrived each day, straining the prison's meager resources to the breaking point. Almost from the start, rations were scarce and of poor quality, and few prisoners had adequate shelter from the summer sun and the winter cold. The only fresh water was what trickled through Stockade Creek, a small stream that flowed through the prison yard into Sweet Water Creek. Waste was often dumped into the water, and downstream, it was used as a latrine for all prisoners. The entire region was soon contaminated, but prisoners continued to drink from it. Health care was nonexistent.

The first commander of Andersonville was John Henry Winder, who oversaw all prisoners held by the Confederacy. Winder died from exhaustion in February 1865 and was succeeded by Henry Wirz, a Swiss born Confederate officer known for his hatred of the Union. According to reports, Wirz did little to alleviate the suffering of his inmates, and the prisoner's increasingly poor conditions took a heavy toll—approximately 13,000 prisoners died there, a mortality rate of about 29 percent.

Sign of the Changing Times **At the end of the war, Henry Wirz became the only Confederate officer to be tried and convicted for war crimes.**

Numerous prisoners who suffered at Andersonville testified against him, as did Clara Barton, who was outraged when she visited the prison site at war's end to identify the dead and missing and see that they received a proper burial. Wirz was held accountable for the conditions at Andersonville, found guilty, and summarily executed. In his own defense, Wirz stated that he simply didn't have food, clothing, or medical supplies to give the prisoners and that his own staff suffered equally as the Confederacy began to crumble.

70.
BATTLEFIELD
MEDICINE UNDER
PAR

MEDICINE WAS STILL IN its infancy during the Civil War, and the wounded and ill paid a horrible price for this lack of knowledge. Ironically, a number of important medical advances were made in the years immediately following the war, but they proved of little use to the poor wretches who found themselves under a battlefield doctor's care. In the eyes of many, those who died in battle were luckier than those who were wounded.

The Minie ball and other bullets and shells used during the Civil War wreaked havoc on the human body. In fact, head and gut wounds caused by Minie balls were almost always fatal. The treatment of choice for broken or lacerated limbs was immediate amputation. The majority of patients were anesthetized with chloroform, ether, nitrous oxide, or, at the very least, a glass of whiskey. When anesthesia was unavailable, a cloth or bullet was placed in the patient's mouth for him to bite on, and he was held down by several strong orderlies while the doctor attended to the damaged limb with a knife and saw. Field doctors quickly became adept at removing limbs with remarkable speed; many could amputate a leg in less than two minutes.

Amputation was only the beginning of a wounded soldier's troubles. If he survived the operation, he would then be transported via ambulance (usually nothing more than a rickety, overcrowded two-wheeled cart or four-wheeled wagon) to the closest army or city hospital. Though his wounds had been treated, chances were better than good that he would soon fall victim to infection or, worse, gangrene. Doctors in the mid-1800s had little understanding of the cause of infection; many thought it was the result of contaminated air, so they seldom did more to clean their surgical tools than wipe them off on a filthy apron before tending to the next patient. Many times, battlefield surgery was done in the open, with a door or wood plank serving as a table and tubs beneath to catch the blood.

As horrible as Civil War surgery was, it was often amazingly successful in saving a wounded soldier's life. According to U.S. Army records, of nearly 29,000 amputations performed during the war, only 7,000 or so patients died as a result.

71.
ANGELS ON THE BATTLEFIELD: CLARA BARTON AND DOROTHEA DIX

CLARA BARTON IS WELL KNOWN as the founder of the American Red Cross, but it was her remarkable humanitarian efforts during the Civil war that established her reputation as the "Angel of the Battlefield." However, Barton's contributions to American society go much farther. She was also an ardent feminist, the first female diplomat, and an important advocate of health and education reform, as well as civil rights.

Barton was born in Massachusetts on Christmas day 1821. She worked first as a schoolteacher and later took a job as a clerk in the U.S. Patent Office in Washington, D.C. It was there that Barton saw the first casualties of the Civil War and witnessed the often inadequate medical treatment they received. She also observed how the wounded frequently went without sufficient food or clothing, a situation she considered unconscionable. Working independently of other relief agencies, Barton, who had no formal medical training, started lobbying to change the horrific conditions of battlefield medicine. One of her first acts was to call on friends in Congress to help improve the health standards within the U.S. military.

On the Homefront At each stop, Barton prepared hot meals for the troops, helped army surgeons in their grisly duty and assisted emergency medical procedures when there was no one else available.

In July 1862, Barton received permission from the U.S. surgeon general to take needed medical supplies directly to the front lines and field hospitals. She risked her life to help the soldiers on the front and made appearances during or immediately following a number of important battles, including Cedar Creek, Second Bull Run, Antietam, and Fredericksburg. She also provided medical aid during the Carolinas campaign and in Virginia during Grant's 1864 offensives, where she was granted an official position with the Army of the James under the command of General Benjamin Butler.

As the war began to wind down, Barton was given a nearly overwhelming task by President Lincoln. He asked her to oversee the search for missing and captured Union soldiers, compile lists of the sick and wounded, and identify the Union dead buried in mass graves at Andersonville Prison and elsewhere. The endeavor took Barton four long years to complete, but her efforts went a long way toward ensuring that Union soldiers who died on the battlefield and in prison were given decent burials and, more importantly, were remembered for their sacrifice.

Dorothea Dix was a nurse of great renown during the Civil War. Prior to the war, Dix had fought to improve the treatment of the mentally ill and the conditions within the nation's prisons. When Fort Sumter was attacked in April 1861, the 59-year-old Dix volunteered her services to the Union and was placed in charge of all female nurses working in army hospitals, a job she held for the duration of the war and for which she received no salary.

One of Dix's biggest jobs was convincing military officials that women could be competent nurses. To ensure that she would not be overwhelmed with young women who only wanted to find a husband, Dix accepted only women who were plain looking and over 30 years old. Those who were chosen were required to wear simple black or brown skirts and were forbidden to wear jewelry. Despite these restrictions, Dix successfully recruited more than 3,000 women to serve as Union army nurses.

72.
WAR DOCTORS:
LITTLE TRAINING,
TOUGH JOB

ONE OF THE BIGGEST MEDICAL problems during the Civil War was the inadequate training received by most doctors. Just prior to the war, the majority of physicians served as apprentices rather than attending medical school, which meant they were woefully unprepared for what they encountered on the battlefield.

Even the doctors who attended the few medical schools in the United States at the time received less than a satisfactory education. In Europe, four-year medical schools were fairly common, and students received a great deal of laboratory training. As a result, European physicians had a far better understanding of the causes and treatment of diseases and infection. By comparison, students in American medical schools trained for less than two years and received almost no clinical experience and very little laboratory instruction. Amazingly, Harvard University—one of the nation's finest universities—d didn't own a single stethoscope or microscope until after the war.

At its onset, the Union army was surprised and shocked by the huge number of casualties the war produced. The federal army had fewer than 100 medical officers at the start of the conflict, and the Confederacy had only 24. By 1865, however, more than 13,000 Union doctors had served in the field and in hospitals. In the Confederacy, approximately 4,000 medical officers and volunteers tended to the wounded. Doctors—almost all of whom were male—were assisted by a large force of volunteer nurses, who gave freely of their time. The number of Southern women who acted as nurses in Confederate hospitals is unknown but believed to be almost as high.

Despite their lack of training and the horrible conditions under which they often worked, Civil War doctors did an astounding job of caring for the sick and wounded. More than 10 million cases of injury and disease were treated in just 48 months, and for the most part, doctors were compassionate and caring individuals who tried to put the concerns of their patients first.

73.
AFRICAN AMERICAN PARTICIPATION AS SOLDIERS

A LARGE NUMBER OF black men saw battle during the Civil War. Bringing blacks into the military was an extraordinarily difficult task, but when they finally received their uniforms and guns, most proved to be exceptionally brave and skilled soldiers.

One might assume that the North would be eager to add black soldiers to its ranks, but such was the not the case. Even though blacks were free in the Northern states, they still faced a tremendous amount of prejudice and bigotry. Many white Northerners secretly—and some not so secretly—disliked blacks. They feared freed slaves would take jobs away from white laborers and drive down wages. Indeed, racial prejudice raised its ugly head in the North numerous times during the war years, and there were several violent and murderous race riots in 1862–63. These riots were sparked primarily by job competition but also by the fear that the emancipation promised by the Civil War would drastically alter everything they knew and held dear. There was a lot of talk in the North about the importance of abolition, and many people fought for it with their very souls, but bigotry still ran rampant.

Conflict of Interest Many Northerners were reluctant to advocate the enlistment of blacks because it was commonly believed that black people had been held in servitude for so long that they were too cowardly to make good soldiers.

Of course, this was false, as evidenced by the fighting skill and bravery of the black regiments that were later formed, but many high-ranking politicians and military officials believed it. Abraham Lincoln, who knew he could not afford to lose the support of border states like Kentucky, was often accused of being slow in advocating the use of black soldiers. When a delegation from Indiana offered Lincoln two regiments of black men to aid the Union effort, Lincoln told them, "If we were to arm [the Negroes], I fear that in a few weeks the arms would be in the hands of the rebels." Lincoln feared that recruiting black soldiers would turn those border states with strong Confederate sympathies against the Union, something he was loath to do.

Not all Union officers believed that blacks were inferior soldiers and sentiments regarding the recruitment of black soldiers slowly changed in the summer of 1862 as the North experienced a number of defeats and morale began to plunge. People were growing weary of the war, and the number of able-bodied white men who enlisted for military service saw a noticeable decline. This forced the government to seriously consider the idea of black recruitment, and in July 1862, Congress passed two acts that opened the door. The first was the Confiscation Act, which gave the president power to "employ as many persons of African descent as he may deem necessary and proper for the suppression of this rebellion." The second was an act that repealed the provisions of an 1792 law barring black men from joining a militia and authorized the active recruitment of free blacks as Union soldiers. It was, however, the president's Emancipation Proclamation, issue in January of 1863 that led to service by 180,000 African American soldiers by the war's end.

74.
THE FAMOUS
MASSACHUSETTS
54TH REGIMENT

THE 54TH MASSACHUSETTS, made famous in the motion picture Glory, was one of the most distinguished black regiments to see combat in the Civil War. The regiment was organized by John Andrew, the abolitionist governor of Massachusetts, immediately following the Emancipation Proclamation, and was composed of 650 African Americans from a number of Northern states.

Andrew was careful to make sure that all of the white officers in charge of the 54th Massachusetts were firm believers in black civil rights. Its commanding officer, Colonel Robert Gould Shaw, came from a vocal abolitionist

Massachusetts family, and he worked hard to ensure that the men under his command were well trained and ready to fight.

After their training was complete, the 54th Massachusetts was assigned to the Department of the South and sent to the South Carolina coast in May 1863. Major General Quincy Gillmore had devised a very risky plan to take back Fort Sumter and capture Charleston. The biggest obstacle was Battery Wagner on the southern tip of Morris Island, which stood little more than a mile from Fort Sumter. The battery was small and fairly isolated, but it was well defended with 1,200 troops and much heavy artillery

Gillmore successfully established a beachhead on the island on July 10, but the fort remained secure. Union forces bombarded the facility with cannon for almost a week, then Gillmore ordered a second assault by 6,000 infantry—with the 54th Massachusetts leading the way. The regiment fought a bloody hand-to-hand battle atop a palmetto parapet before being pushed back. Colonel Shaw was killed by a bullet through the heart, and nearly 40 percent of his regiment was slaughtered in the failed assault. The bodies of the dead, including Shaw, were buried on the beach in a mass grave.

Despite the failure of the assault on Battery Wagner, the noble efforts of the 54th Massachusetts contributed greatly to bolstering the image of black soldiers. The regiment's surviving members, under the command of Colonel Edward Hallowell, stayed in South Carolina for another year, then returned home to a hero's celebration.

75.
ETHNIC MAKEUP
OF THE CIVIL WAR

SOLDIERS FROM A WIDE variety of ethnic backgrounds participated in the Civil War. Of the approximately two million Union soldiers,
nearly a quarter were foreign born. Approximately 175,000 were German, 150,000 were Irish, and 50,000 were English or Canadian. Native
Americans also fought on both sides, as did a number of Hispanics and
Scandinavians, as well as other nationalities.

Irish Americans, in particular, played an integral role in the war. The
nation had seen an immigration boom between the 1830s and the 1850s, and
New York and Boston both contained large Irish enclaves. According to the
1860 census, more than 1.5 million Americans claimed to be from Ireland.
The number of soldiers of Irish descent in the Union army is well verified,
but statistics regarding the Confederacy are almost unknown. Still, Southern

On the Homefront **Immigration continued almost unabated in the
North throughout the war, and many newcomers from foreign lands
showed their gratitude by joining the Union army within months of their
arrival.**

songs of the era suggest a strong regional Irish influence. In the Union, some of the most notable regiments were Irish, such as Thomas Meagher's Irish Brigade, which went into battle with a green flag containing a large golden harp in its center.

A large number of Germans also immigrated to the United States in the decades preceding the war, and most of those who ended up in military service fought for the Union. Most German immigrants (as well as Austrians and Dutch) made their homes in areas that reminded them of their homeland, places such as Pennsylvania, Delaware, and Virginia. When the war broke out, they enlisted without hesitation, and many German Americans rose to positions of great importance within the Union army.

The participation of Native Americans in the Civil War cannot be overlooked. The war years were difficult for these indigenous people, most of whom were struggling for their own independence and autonomy. Some tribes, such as the Cherokee, participated directly in the war; others, especially those in the East, decided on an individual basis whether to get involved. In the West and elsewhere, many tribes realized that the war offered an opportunity for them to reclaim lands that had been taken from them, because it meant fewer federal soldiers overseeing their territories.

According to government records, approximately 3,600 Native Americans served in the Union army during the war.

76.
CHRONICLING
THE CIVIL WAR

THE CIVIL WAR WAS one of the first wars to be extensively covered in the press on both sides. Newspaper and magazine journalists from the North, the South, and overseas were given amazing freedom to follow armies, observe battles, and talk with commanders. The resulting stories—while often showing a decided bias—have helped historians understand exactly what happened during the war and why.

Newspapers and magazines reported the war in two ways: through on-site coverage of battles and other important events and through editorials stating the publication's position on a particular subject.

In the North, the majority of newspapers, but not all, shared the abolitionist sentiment expressed by the government. Some papers sympathized with the Confederate cause and stated so vociferously. In the South, the vast majority of papers were proslavery and anti-Union. But again, there was a small number of dissenting voices.

Modern newspapers frequently carry blistering attacks on public officials and government policy, and such was the case during the Civil War as well. Abraham Lincoln and Jefferson Davis were often pilloried in the press for their actions and policies, and their military leaders also found themselves subject to ridicule and attack, especially when they didn't win. Indeed, military success always seemed to play a role in whether the government was perceived positively or negatively.

As with combat journalists today, reporters covering field action risked their lives to get the story. Daily newspapers and weekly news magazines such as *Harper's Weekly* and *Leslie's* sent reporters, photographers, and artists out by the dozens to cover the action, and many lost their lives in the process. Photography was still in its infancy, so most newspapers and magazines relied on sketch artists to capture the essence of a particular event or scene in a drawing, which would be used to illustrate the reporters' words. Thanks to these unsung heroes, no aspect of the Civil War was left unexamined and our understanding of this very unique conflict is probably better than in any previous American war.

77.
MATTHEW BRADY, THE FATHER OF CONTEMPORARY PHOTOJOURNALISM

THE CIVIL WAR WAS covered at every angle by a literal army of journalists, artists, and photographers—nearly 500 by some estimates. So thorough was media coverage of the conflict that opposing generals sometimes learned more from enemy newspapers than from spy reports.

William T. Sherman, who found himself the frequent subject of journalistic ridicule, was not a fan of the press. He once noted, "Reporters print their limited and tainted observations as the history of events they neither see nor comprehend." Others, however, avidly followed the war in their favorite newspapers.

The public also saw the war in the numerous photographs taken on the battlefield. Matthew Brady has been called the father of contemporary photojournalism, and with good reason; the photographs taken by him and his staff chronicled for the first time a war in progress and placed a human face on the horrible consequences of warfare.

The photographic process was extremely slow, and exposures were typically long, which explains why there are very few actual battle scenes—

moving bodies photographed simply as blurs. Brady's cameras were set up next to his black wagon and aimed at the scene or persons to be photographed. An assistant would bring out a special 8-by-10 inch glass plate that had been stored in a dust-proof box and cleaned immediately before use. The plate would be inserted into the camera exposed, then rushed into the wagon for development.

During this period, Brady's eyesight began to fail, so he hired a staff of photographers to continue his work. Few, however, received the credit due them, and Brady's name appeared on many photographs that he did not shoot. Several of the photographers under Brady's employ eventually went off on their own, seeking fame and fortune by covering the war for newspapers, magazines, and historical archives.

Brady and his staff managed to produce more than 3,500 photographs covering nearly every aspect of the war, including camp life, military portraits, and scenes of the aftermath of battle. Brady realized the importance of composition in a photograph and encouraged his staff to pose live soldiers as if they were going off to battle and to rearrange corpses for better visual effect.

78.
ESPIONAGE
DURING THE WAR

BOTH THE NORTH AND THE SOUTH had a network of spies in enemy territory whose job was to ferret out information on battle plans, the number of forces, as well as other information. Some spies were more effective than others. Rose O'Neal Greenhow, for example, was a member of Washington society, a friend of numerous Northern politicians—and a Confederate spy. She sent information on Union plans to Confederate military leaders via coded messages transported by women on horseback.

Even more famous was Confederate spy Belle Boyd, the Mata Hari of her time. According to lore, Boyd decided to become a spy for the Confederacy at age 17, after Union soldiers ransacked her family's Virginia home. Boyd operated from a Front Royal hotel owned by her father, and was especially helpful during Stonewall Jackson's Shenandoah Valley campaign in the spring of 1862. She provided important information regarding the movement of Union troops, as well as other secrets she managed to extract from Union officers by using her feminine wiles. Boyd delivered her reports via bold nighttime rides through enemy territory.

Sign of the Changing Times Boyd proved so helpful to the Confederate cause that Jackson named her an honorary aide-de-camp, and she became known throughout the South as "La Belle Rebelle."

Boyd eventually came to the attention of authorities in Washington and was arrested at least six times. In June 1862, Boyd was placed in a Washington jail after being betrayed by one of her lovers, but she continued to aid the Confederacy by tossing rubber balls containing detailed notes from her jail cell window to an operative on the street below. Boyd was released in a prisoner exchange after four weeks of incarceration but found herself behind bars yet again the following year, this time for five months. Boyd was released in December 1863 after contracting typhoid fever; she immediately went to Europe. She told people she was traveling abroad to recuperate from her illness, but in fact, she was delivering letters from Jefferson Davis to the British government.

Boyd tried to return to the South aboard a Confederate blockade runner, but the boat was stopped by a Union ship. The vessel's captain, Samuel Hardringe, fell in love with Boyd and helped her escape to Canada. They later married in England, but Hardringe, who had resigned his commission in the Union navy, died shortly after. When the war ended, Boyd published her autobiography and spent several decades entertaining lecture audiences in both the North and the South with tales of her adventures as a war spy. Belle Boyd died in 1900 while on tour.

79.
WOMEN AND CHILDREN IN THE LINE OF FIRE?

CONTRARY TO POPULAR BELIEF, the Civil War was not fought only by adult males. Women and children also participated in the conflict in a variety of capacities, often giving their lives for a cause they deeply believed in.

Many women did their part by traveling with soldiers as members of the so-called "soapsuds brigade," whose sole job was to clean the clothes of military units. It was a difficult, physically challenging job, but the soldiers deeply appreciated and respected the women who kept them in clean uniforms. In most cases, members of the "soapsuds brigade" were the only women given official status in camp. Others, including officers' wives, were simply labeled "camp followers." In the Union army, each company was permitted four laundresses. Many washerwomen were married to soldiers and lived with their husbands in the area of camp commonly known as "suds row." If not married to a soldier, washerwomen were expected to be at least somehow related to a member of the unit. A washerwoman named Hannah O'Neil, for example, followed her son, who was a member of Company H of the 1st Minnesota Volunteer Infantry.

Far more rare were women who followed their loved ones into battle as more than washerwomen. A few military units "adopted" women as mascots or aides, and these women faced the same dangers as the male soldiers.

Rarer still—but more common than many historians originally believed—were women who disguised their gender in order to enlist and fight at the front on equal standing with male soldiers. Pulling off such a feat was not easy, but many women did so successfully, slipping through the enlistment process and fooling their fellow soldiers for months and even years. The majority of women who are known to have done this fought with the same bravery and zeal as their male counterparts. Those exposed because of injury or illness were either honorably discharged or merely dismissed, depending on their commanding officer. Many who were lauded for their military service drew veterans' pensions following the war.

On the Homefront Children—that is, boys under the age of 18—also saw quite a bit of military service. Many lied about their age when enlisting; others were adopted as mascots by various military units. The exact number of underage soldiers is unknown, but some historians say the figure could be as high as 400,000.

Many children were able to slip into the armed forces because recruiters were eager to fill quotas and usually didn't question boys who looked at least 18 years old. However, even boys who were obviously underage succeeded in getting in; many were assigned as regimental musicians.

Probably the most famous child to participate in the war is Johnny Clem, who became a legend in the Northern press. Clem ran away from home in 1861 at age nine to join a Union army regiment that had traveled through his hometown in Ohio. He was turned away but later joined another unit and served as its drummer boy; he also performed other camp chores. The soldiers took a liking to Clem and chipped in to pay him a proper soldier's wage—$13 a month.

Clem was first immortalized in the press following the Battle of Shiloh in April 1862, during which his drum was apparently destroyed. The Union press started referring to Clem as "Johnny Shiloh" and identified him as the subject of a popular song and stage play. Officially enrolled in the army, complete with a miniature, hand-carved musket, Clem received additional press coverage as "The Drummer Boy of Chickamauga." During that battle, Clem allegedly shot and captured a Confederate soldier who tried to take him prisoner. Whether the story is true or not remains uncertain, but it helped make Clem a national hero.

Despite his young age, Clem was captured once and wounded twice over the course of the war and rose to the rank of lance sergeant before his 14th birthday. A few years later, Clem tried to enroll in West Point but was denied admission because he lacked a formal education. As a result of a direct appeal from President Grant, he was then given a commission as second lieutenant and placed in command of a unit of black soldiers. He made the military his life career, retiring as a major general shortly before the start of World War I. Clem died in 1937.

PART FIVE

THE HOMEFRONT

THE CIVIL WAR WAS AN ALL-ENCOMPASSING EVENT THAT touched the lives of almost every American. Whether you lived in the backwoods of Kentucky or a thriving eastern metropolis such as New York City, the effects of the war were pervasive and inescapable.

An astounding number of families on both sides of the conflict watched fathers, sons, and neighbors march off to battle, and many grieved when their loved ones and friends did not return. But even those families who didn't have members actively fighting in the war still felt its influence in myriad ways—raging battles only miles away, participation in the manufacture of products for the war machine, raucous debates over the causes of the conflict, or the pinch of increasingly higher taxes as the governments of the North and South struggled to finance their individual efforts. All Americans, whether Union or Confederate by sentiment, experienced the war every moment of every day.

80.
EFFECTS,
FOR EVERY
AMERICAN

WHILE BATTLES RAGED AND lives were lost by the tens of thousands, life continued in relative normalcy for those outside its direct sphere of influence. Machinists worked, farmers tended their land, and families did their best to enjoy the simple pleasures. People went to plays and concerts, participated in sports such as baseball, entertained one another with fine parties and casual picnics, and lived each day in the desperate hope that night would fall without the bearing of bad news. Some families were luckier than others.

The Civil War is the largest military event ever fought on American soil, and the heaviest fighting occurred in the Southern states. Maintaining a semblance of normal daily living was much more difficult there than in the Northern states, which, for the most part, managed to get through the war without experiencing the devastating ravages of battle. Those living in the Confederacy were hopeful at the beginning that the war would be over quickly, that the Union would accept their proclamation of independence, and that they would soon be free to live their lives as they so wished. History, of course, shows that this was not the case. The war fell heavily upon the citizens of the Confederacy, and millions watched helplessly as family members perished, everything they worked for was destroyed, and the normalcy of life became a distant memory. Indeed, during the final devastating year of the war, life was anything but ordinary within the Confederate States of America. Its army was in disarray, its soldiers and citizens were on the brink of starvation, and any hope of freedom seemed little more than a pipe dream. Yet its people persevered.

81.
AMERICA ON THE EVE OF DESTRUCTION

AS NOTED EARLIER, THE United States of America was in the throes of remarkable growth and prosperity during the three decades prior to the onset of the Civil War. The nation's population, encouraged by seemingly endless expansion, multiplied by leaps and bounds. In fact, by 1860, the nation was home to nearly 32 million people (including four million slaves). Since 1810, the American population had grown four times faster than Europe's and almost six times the world average. And why not? There was plenty of room, plenty of food, and plenty of work for anyone who wanted it. America was, indeed, the land of opportunity.

In the decades preceding the war, as well as the war years themselves, most Americans continued to live in rural areas—that is, towns with fewer than 2,500 people.

Sign of the Changing Times But the urban population was growing by leaps and bounds as people headed to burgeoning cities to seek their fortunes.

The rate of urbanization during this period was the highest in American history, with the city population growing three times faster than the rural population in the five decades between 1810 and 1860. Industry flourished in the North while agriculture, particularly cotton, continued to dominate the Southern economy.

Americans witnessed a huge evolution in lifestyle in the decades prior to the Civil War. A network of canals, highways, and railroads made transportation faster and easier (and dramatically reduced the cost of shipping goods) throughout the Northern states and into the South and West, and the telegraph made transcontinental communication almost instantaneous.

Of equal importance was the rise of the middle class, which took advantage of dramatic advances in manufacturing. In the past, the manufacture of common goods relied for the most part on specialization. Talented craftsmen made everything by hand, from shoes to guns to farm equipment. But the American industrial revolution, with its emphasis on interchangeable parts and factory assembly, quickly changed the way Americans shopped. Craftsmen were still in high demand, especially in regions where the results of mass production had not yet reached in volume, but more and more Americans bought factory or pre-made goods simply because the price was so affordable.

A particularly good example of this phenomenon is housing. At the beginning of the nineteenth century, there were three different types of housing: rough-hewn log cabins, which tended to be drafty as well as austere; homes made from brick or stone; and homes made from fastened, heavy timbers cut to shape by carpenters. Log homes were the least expensive and easiest homes to make, but most middle- and upper-income families wanted something nicer. However, the craftsmen necessary to build stone or timber homes were in short supply, so the wait could be long.

The answer came in the form of balloon-frame houses, homes made from machine-sawed boards fastened together with industrial nails. Once the frame was up, factory-made siding, shingles, doors, and windows completed the structure. The construction of a balloon-frame home didn't take nearly as long or cost nearly as much as one made from stone or hand-hewn timber, and the resulting structure was both attractive and sturdy. The first balloon-frame homes were built in Chicago and Rochester, New York, in the 1830s and quickly revolutionized the housing industry in this country. Such advances greatly improved the lifestyle of many Americans.

82.
CHANGING ROLES, FAMILY LIFE

THE CIVIL WAR WAS especially difficult on the family unit, which tended to be close knit and often extended. In most families, the husband and the eldest sons were the primary breadwinners, and it was a great loss when they had to go off to war. This was especially true among middle-class families, in which wives and mothers often had little experience providing for their families. A farmer's wife knew how to hold down the family stake in her husband's absence (though the labor issue was often a problem), but city women were in a much more difficult position.

Women of the era had an indomitable spirit, however, and they drew from deep reserves of strength and ingenuity when it came to supporting their families. Those who had been sheltered their entire lives, which was common, often found the transition traumatic, but they persevered as never before, falling back on whatever marketable skills they could muster and refusing to take no for an answer. In many ways, Civil War wives were the forebears of World War II's "Rosie the Riveter" and the trend-setting feminists of the 1960s and 1970s.

In addition to the financial hardship, the families of wounded veterans often had to face tremendous psychological pain. Many soldiers returned home suffering from what today would be diagnosed as posttraumatic stress disorder, and they and their loved ones had few places to turn for help. Psychiatric therapy was unheard of back then, so most families turned to close friends and clergy for solace and guidance (which more often than not consisted of the statement, "Just try to be patient"). Many women, initially ecstatic when their husbands returned home, watched their lives slowly crumble as they realized the rest of their years would be spent tending to their husbands' permanent wounds. More than one woman found that she couldn't tolerate her postwar family existence and fled for a better life elsewhere.

On the home front, many women participated in military assistance and relief efforts, such as sewing bees, food drives, and medical collections.

Not only did these activities help provide soldiers with desperately appreciated items they probably wouldn't have been able to find elsewhere, but they gave the women a sense of unity and purpose. Families and soldiers also kept bonds strong by writing long letters back and forth. Nothing made a soldier's day like a letter from his loving wife, and vice versa. Thankfully, many of these letters have been passed down from generation to generation, creating a rich tapestry of information and opinion that has provided contemporary historians with deep insight into the war.

Northern families lost a great many loved ones over the course of the war and experienced their share of problems and grief, but it can be argued that Southern families suffered far more. In the North, only the Gettysburg and the Sharpsburg campaigns brought the war to the doorstep of Union civilians. In the South, the threat of warfare was almost a daily occurrence. Numerous Southern towns and cities were destroyed over the course of the war, and the impact on the Confederate civilian population was enormous in virtually all areas. In many regions, it took all the coping skills families could muster to survive each day.

83.
IDEOLOGICAL RIFT DIVIDES FAMILIES

THE CIVIL WAR DIVIDED not only the nation but also individual families. School children have long been taught that the conflict pitted brother against brother, and this is absolutely true. In fact, the ideological rift at the center of the war went all the way to the White House; four of Lincoln's brothers-in-law served in the Confederate army. One of them, Ben Hardin Helm, turned down Lincoln's personal offer of a commission in the Union army so that he could fight for the Confederates. He eventually rose to the rank of general. Helm was killed in the Battle of Chickamaugua.

Certainly the Lincolns weren't the only family to experience the pain of mixed loyalties.

Henry Clay of Kentucky, for example, who was dead by the time the war occurred, had grandsons who served on both sides. And John J. Crittenden, the former governor and U.S. Senator from Kentucky who tried to

Conflict of Interest **Many families, especially those from the border states, watched brothers march off in opposite directions, with the very real possibility that they would have to shoot at each other.**

prevent the war in 1860 with a compromise known as the Crittenden Plan, had sons in both blue and gray.

Relatives rarely ended up actually facing each other in battle, though there are numerous tales of wartime encounters, some of which are clearly apocryphal. One of the most touching stories is that of Major A.M. Lea, who was part of the Confederate force that captured the USS *Harriet Lane* during a naval battle off Galveston, Texas. When Lea's party boarded the Union ship, he found his son—a Union lieutenant—dying on its deck.

The duel between the Confederate ironclad *Virginia* and the Union ironclad *Monitor* also had a family connection. McKean Buchanan, the brother of *Virginia* commander Franklin Buchanan, was aboard a Union ship sunk during the battle.

84.
CITY LIFE,
FAR FROM THE
BATTLEFIELD

WHEN WE TALK ABOUT city life during the Civil War, we're talking primarily about the North. The vast majority of the nation's largest cities were located in the Northern states, with the South lagging far behind.

One of the reasons for this was the huge influx of foreign immigrants—primarily from Ireland and Germany—who poured into the nation in the decades prior to the war. While many new arrivals spread out to settle in regions that reminded them of home, the majority stayed in the cities—New York, Chicago, Boston, and other metropolitan areas—in the hope of finding well-paying jobs in the many factories and businesses located there. This influx would continue as the war raged, making many American cities some of the most populous in the world.

What was city life like during the Civil War? In many respects, it wasn't that different from city life today. There were the very rich, the very poor, and the many in between. The poor tended to live in tenements; the rich lived in fine homes that often resembled palaces. The captains of industry, many of whom had grown rich off of the hard work of immigrant labor, usually lived in and around the cities in which their factories were located. That way, they could keep a close eye on their businesses without having to travel very far.

Things were a bit more relaxed in the largest cities of the South, such as New Orleans, Richmond, Savannah, and Atlanta. The pace of the Southern states in general was much slower, a phenomenon that often baffled hardworking visiting Northerners before the war. One reason, of course, was that much of the region's hard labor was performed by slaves, giving its wealthier citizens plenty of free time in which to relax and indulge their personal passions.

Southern cities were bustling but not overly crowded. Just prior to the beginning of the Civil War, Charleston, Richmond, and Savannah each had fewer than 40,000 citizens. Only New Orleans was comparable to the largest Northern cities, with a population of around 150,000. People traveled by carriage, cart, or horseback and very often lived on the outskirts of the city itself. And as in the North, entertainment was ample and diverse, including stage productions, musical concerts, and other shows.

85.
SURVIVING
ON THE FARM

FARM LIFE IN THE MIDDLE of the nineteenth century was hard work, even with the many labor-saving devices that had become available as a result of the industrial revolution. Farmers typically rose with the sun, had a quick breakfast, then tended to their livestock. Even small farms usually had at least one cow and perhaps some hogs, chickens, and goats. All provided food for the family and perhaps a small amount to sell at market. Once the animals had been fed, the farmer would spend the rest of his day tending to his crops, which varied greatly from one region to another. In the Midwest, wheat, corn, potatoes, and other staples were common. In the South, cotton was king on most plantations, but smaller farms usually grew food crops such as corn, rice, and sugar, as well as indigo and tobacco, which even then were lucrative cash crops.

Farming communities in both regions tended to be fairly close knit, with farmers coming to the aid of others when necessary. Most farmers used hired help to tend the land, though smaller farms were typically family affairs, especially if the family included several strong boys. Despite the common notion regarding slavery in the South, most small- to middle-sized Southern farms did not use slaves, because of the high cost of purchase and maintenance; slaves were more a luxury for wealthy plantation owners.

Unlike their overly protected city sisters, however, farm wives tended to be robust in nature and unafraid of hard labor. When their husbands went off to war, they picked up the hoe and plow and, without complaint, went to work. It was seldom a question of yes or no; for most farmers' wives, it was a simple issue of survival.

On the Homefront **As the war depleted the nation's male population, farmers' wives in both the North and the South suddenly found themselves the heads of their households.**

Farmers often suffered greatly during the Civil War, especially in the South. They usually lived far from town, which made them easy targets for marauders and invading forces, especially those in desperate need of food. Hungry Confederate soldiers begged for whatever a farmer could spare, but Union soldiers were seldom as considerate. Pillaging was discouraged by most officers, but the rule was difficult to enforce, and Union soldiers often took whatever they wanted and destroyed crops and livestock simply to keep them from falling into Confederate hands. Sadly, many farmers were unjustly punished by this reasoning, and it wasn't uncommon for a fleeing farmer to return to his home only to find it burned to the ground. This was especially true during Sherman's march to the sea and his campaign through the Carolinas.

86.
LIFESTYLE OF THE LANDED GENTRY, PLANTATION LIFE

CONTRARY TO POPULAR BELIEF, which has been fueled by movies such as Gone with the Wind, the South was not one huge collection of large plantations. In truth, there were far more small- and middle-sized farms—most of which were tended without slaves. However, it's the easy lifestyle of the landed gentry that has become so firmly embedded in the public consciousness.

The Deep South was home to the majority of plantations, as they are recalled today—large, almost palatial homes overseeing hundreds and often thousands of acres of prime farmland, tended by slaves. Louisiana and Virginia both contained a large number of plantations, most of which grew cotton, tobacco, indigo, and rice. But plantations could be found in almost all of the Confederate states. Indeed, the plantation embodied the Southern sensibility and lifestyle in the eyes of most Northerners, even if they had never seen one.

The treatment of slaves varied greatly among plantation owners. Some were strict to the point of brutality, administering severe punishment for the slightest infraction and running the home more by fear than respect. But for the most part, planters took relatively good care of their slaves, who were viewed as an expensive investment (a capable farmhand could cost more than $1,000 at auction). Punishment was doled out where appropriate, but minor infractions were often ignored. Many plantation owners also gave their slaves a small piece of land to farm for themselves and sometimes even paid them a small wage or allowance with which they could buy personal items. Of course, that's not to infer that the life of a slave was pleasant. Even under the best circumstances, slaves were still considered nothing more than property, and even the best-treated slave still dreamed of freedom.

87.
SLAVERY IN THE BIBLE?

NINETEENTH-CENTURY AMERICA found itself in the midst of a religious upheaval. Prior to 1830, the majority of white Americans were of British heritage and Protestant in their beliefs. By 1830, however, the floodgates of immigration had been thrown wide open and tens of thousands of Irish and German immigrants made their way across the Atlantic. More than two-thirds of these new settlers were Catholic, a situation that greatly alarmed many Protestant Americans and resulted in an increase in nativist organizations. Sadly, this anti-Catholic bias would last for decades.

Americans, for the most part, were a deeply religious people. The Protestant work ethic was alive and well during the Civil War era, and it was the rare individual in either the North or the South who didn't attend church on a regular basis. In addition, evangelists traveled the countryside preaching fire and brimstone at every stop. The sins of alcohol was an especially popular subject of sermons, and many regions experienced a noticeable drop in alcohol consumption and an increase in productivity after a visit by a particularly eloquent preacher.

Conflict of Interest In the North, the evil inherent in slavery was also a popular subject, and abolitionist preachers used the pulpit to stir up anti-slavery sentiment. Southerners countered by quoting scripture they felt actually condoned slavery.

Genesis 9:25–27, for example, was often used as justification for enslaving blacks. The passage quotes Noah, who has been angered by his son Ham, cursing all of Ham's descendants: "a slave shall he be to his brothers." According to the Bible, Ham fathered four sons, who gave rise to the southern tribes of the earth, including all of the people of Africa. Many Southerners also defended the institution with the argument that slavery was actually good for blacks because it enabled them to be converted to Christianity and thus go to heaven.

PART SIX

THE END OF THE CONFLICT, RECONSTRUCTION, AND THE WAR'S LEGACY

THE CIVIL WAR ENDED ALMOST FOUR YEARS TO THE day after it started—sort of. Most people assume that hostilities between the North and the South concluded immediately with Robert E. Lee's surrender to Ulysses S. Grant on April 9, 1865, but sporadic fighting continued on various fronts for another two and a half months.

88.
AN END IN SIGHT

IN THE END, LEE'S surrender truly did signal the final defeat of the Confederacy. It was the last of a long line of falling dominoes that included Grant's hard-fought triumph at Petersburg; the fall of Richmond; Sherman's victories at Atlanta, Savannah, and through the Carolinas; and Philip Sheridan's lengthy Shenandoah Valley campaign. All of these events took a huge toll on the Confederacy's already weakened fighting force, which had been hit hard by a lack of necessary supplies and the plummeting morale of its soldiers, a growing number of whom deserted during the war's waning days.

Amazingly, Confederate President Jefferson Davis had plans to continue the war even as he and his cabinet fled Richmond to the din of approaching Union forces echoing behind them. An angry Confederate to the bitter end, Davis carried with him up to the moment of his capture the belief that the Confederacy would prevail if given enough time, but he was pretty much alone in that sentiment.

On the Homefront   By April 1865, the Confederacy had clearly lost
its ability to fight, and no amount of rally cries could revive it. Most
of Davis's closest advisors and associates knew the cause had been lost
months before, but none could convince Davis to bargain for peace.

A number of diverse factors contributed to the Confederacy's ultimate
demise. Foremost was the combined forces of Grant and Sherman, who
brought down the South with a divide-and-conquer strategy. While Grant
forced Lee's hand at Petersburg, Sherman took Atlanta then effectively split
the South in half with his march to the sea and into the Carolinas. The
combined attacks pushed the already battered and much smaller Confederate
army to the point where it could no longer defend itself, ensuring a Union
victory.

The state of the Southern economy was also a contributing factor. The
gravity of the situation became evident more than a year before the war officially ended, and it only got worse as the conflict progressed. Its economy
close to ruin, the fledgling nation had neither the credit nor the cash to buy
foreign goods for its army or its people. As a result, consumer goods became
increasingly scarce and outrageously expensive, and the army was finally
forced to literally beg the civilian populace—most of whom had long grown
tired of the war—for food, clothing, and other essential items. Of course, this
situation did little to instill confidence in the Confederacy.

Able-bodied men also grew short in numbers as the war went on, forcing the military to take almost anyone willing to fight, including underage

boys and old men. At the beginning, prisoner exchanges allowed both sides to maintain strong numbers, but the eventual Union cessation of the program hit the Confederacy hard; all of a sudden, tens of thousands of Southern soldiers were languishing in Union prisons. The huge number of casualties in many of the major battles also severely depleted Confederate forces. In many cases, the actual number of Union casualties was higher, but the overall percentage was smaller. In other words, the South lost fewer men on average but took a harder hit with the number it did lose. Not surprisingly, Confederate recruitment drives during the final year of the war provided fewer and fewer soldiers willing to lay down their lives for a cause many were starting to believe was hopeless.

Another factor in the defeat of the Confederacy was its inability to receive formal international recognition, particularly from England and France. These and other countries assisted the Confederacy in a number of ways, but they ultimately refused to grant it official status as an independent nation. This meant that the Confederacy was unable to get much-needed loans with which to buy supplies to maintain its war machine. This, compounded with the Union blockade of Southern ports, dealt the Confederacy a serious blow.

The international eye was on the Confederacy from the very beginning of the war, and early Confederate victories suggested that recognition might be forthcoming. After all, the South had a lot to offer the international market by way of food, textiles, and other goods. However, the Confederacy was unable to maintain its momentum, and the foreign powers finally sided with the sure thing—the Union. Of course, the Confederacy's ill-fated 1861 European cotton embargo didn't help matters.

89.
THE FINAL
BATTLES

IIISTORIANS COULD EASILY SPEND years trying to determine which specific battle or event was the loosened lynchpin that brought down the South. But for all intents and purposes, the death of the Confederacy started at Petersburg, Virginia, in June 1864.

Petersburg was an important city. It contained communication and supply lines that were vital to the Confederate capital of Richmond, which was just 20 miles away. This made it an important target for Grant, who knew that when Petersburg fell, Richmond would be next. And with Richmond—the heart of the Confederacy—would go the war.

For Lee, calamity came in late March 1865. Realizing that Petersburg was a lost cause, Lee developed a daring plan that called for him and his

Sign of the Changing Times   However, as noted earlier, Petersburg was not an easy Union victory. Defending Confederate forces under Lee, though relatively small, were well entrenched. Despite Grant's larger numbers, it took a grueling 10-month siege to bring the city under Union control.

troops to flee the city, hook up with Johnston to stop Sherman's assault, then return to take on Grant. It was a bold ploy that might actually have worked had Lee a sufficient number of men, though even with his small army, he had no other choice.

Just before daylight on March 25, 1865, Confederate forces under General John Gordon attacked Union-held Fort Stedman, which lay directly east of Petersburg. The surprise assault was a success, and the rebel forces pushed on to the Union secondary line. If they could break the line and hold it, Lee's army could push through and on to North Carolina, where Johnston continued to nip at Sherman's heels. Unfortunately for Lee, the Union forces rallied with a mighty counterattack that destroyed the Confederate front. By midmorning, Lee's forces had been pushed back at a loss of nearly 5,000 men. With that, Grant—assisted by Philip Sheridan's cavalry—made a major push against Lee's right flank in the hope of preventing Lee's escape to the south. On March 29, a full corps attacked Lee's right while Sheridan led a corps of cavalry and infantry in a wide sweep toward the small town of Five Forks on the Confederate right. Sheridan knew that if he could get behind Lee's army, he could stop it in its tracks and effectively end the war that day.

But Lee wasn't about to go down without a fight. He quickly realized what was happening and sent troops under George Pickett to oppose Sheridan's assault. Pickett managed to stop Sheridan at Dinwiddie Courthouse, just short of Five Forks, on March 31. But Sheridan wasn't defeated; he merely waited for reinforcements. Grant sent him a corps, under General Gouverneur Kemble Warren; it arrived shortly.

The ensuing battle was hard fought, with Sheridan, atop his horse, loudly rallying his troops, hell-bent on stopping Lee at all costs.

Sheridan's goal was the Southside Railway, a Confederate central supply line. It wouldn't happen on that first day of fighting, but Sheridan's forces did manage to all but annihilate Pickett's army and take the town of Five Forks. Grant cabled Lincoln that Five Forks was under Union control and that Petersburg was next. Lincoln contacted the press, which carried the news under huge headlines. The end of the war was within the Union's grasp.

On April 2, Grant launched an all-out assault along the Confederate line defending Petersburg. Artillery battered the rebel forces, softening the line and killing many. Then the guns stopped, and Union infantry attacked in a huge wave that eventually tore a hole in the middle of the Confederate line. The rebels fought with all they had, but they were simply outnumbered and outgunned. Lee knew that Petersburg was lost and made plans to abandon the city. He wired Jefferson Davis that Richmond could no longer be protected and encouraged Davis and his cabinet to flee the capital as quickly as possible. Then Lee took his remaining army of hungry, ill-equipped men and headed west, with the intention of joining Joseph Johnston's army.

90.
THE HAMPTON ROADS CONFERENCE CALLS FOR PEACE

THE CIVIL WAR ALMOST ended two months before it actually did. On February 3, 1865, President Abraham Lincoln and Secretary of State William Seward met with representatives of the Confederate government aboard a steamboat in Hampton Roads, Virginia, at the mouth of the James River.

The peace conference was conceived by newspaper editor Francis P. Blair Sr., who hoped that the two sides would be willing to settle their differences and join forces to secure American interests in Mexico, which was under the control of Maximillian, an Austrian who had been placed in power by Napoleon III and the French government. Blair first consulted Jefferson Davis with the idea and then, after receiving permission from Lincoln, set the meeting in motion.

Davis knew that the chances of hammering out an actual peace treaty were slim, but he felt that standing up to the North would help rally the Confederacy during this especially dire time. Lincoln agreed to the meeting in the hope that a peace treaty would help avoid the punitive Reconstruction that it was feared would come in the wake of a decisive Confederate defeat.

Lincoln and Seward spent several hours talking with the Confederate representatives, who included Vice President Alexander Hamilton Stephens, ex-Supreme Court Justice John Campbell, and former Secretary of State Robert Hunter. However, the talks fell apart when the Confederacy refused to consider Lincoln's demand for complete restoration of the Union and the abolition of slavery.

Davis used the meeting to his advantage, printing up Lincoln's demands and distributing them throughout the South as a way of stimulating Confederate patriotism and rallying the fledgling nation's flagging spirits. At the same time, radical Republicans were outraged at Lincoln's plan for mild Reconstruction and immediately started the groundwork for far more severe punishments for the rebellious South.

91.
THE SURRENDER
OF ROBERT E. LEE

ROBERT E. LEE'S ARMY got a one-day jump on Ulysses S. Grant's pursuing forces, abandoning Petersburg for Danville, Virginia, where Jefferson Davis hoped to reinstate the Confederate government and keep the war going. Lee knew the continuation of hostilities was futile, but as a professional soldier, he couldn't bring himself to question his commander-in-chief.

On the night of April 3, 1865, Lee's army found itself in Amelia Courthouse, a little more than 20 miles from Petersburg. Lee had hoped to find rations for his starving men, but there wasn't a single morsel to be had. Desperate to move on, he had no choice but to remain an extra day while scouts foraged the countryside in search of food. This cost Lee his one-day head start and placed him and his men in great jeopardy.

The area was swarming with Union troops. Following very close behind were three corps of Union infantry, marching a few miles south of Lee on a parallel course. And on the night of April 4, some of Sheridan's cavalry made a tentative move into Amelia Courthouse. Lee knew he couldn't stay; to do so would be folly.

The forage wagons upon which Lee had pinned his hopes returned nearly empty on April 5. This meant that his men would have to march on empty stomachs, something they had been forced to do for far too long. After another brief delay so that additional Confederate forces under General George Thomas Anderson and General Richard Ewell could join him, Lee ordered his army to move out—only to find his path blocked by Union infantry and cavalry.

Rather than directly face the larger Federal force, Lee shifted west toward Farmville, where he hoped to receive food and provisions for his men from nearby Lynchburg. The night march there took a heavy toll on Lee's hungry, exhausted men, many of whom stumbled out of the walking columns and were never seen again. And as always, Federal forces continued to harass the Confederates as they slowly made their way. Grant dogged Lee with unflagging determination, pressing closer and closer, unwilling to let his esteemed foe escape yet again. The end was close, and both men knew it.

On April 6, Union forces overwhelmed John Gordon's army, which was covering the Confederate trains, at the small town of Sayler's Creek. During that battle, federal soldiers captured the majority of Lee's supply wagons and, even more heartbreaking, decimated the corps led by Anderson and Ewell. Lee's army took a huge hit during the battle, losing more than 7,000 men and reducing his force to just 15,000 soldiers armed with only muskets and sabers. Opposing them was 80,000 Union infantry and cavalry.

The following day, Lee's army stumbled into Farmville, where they received food for the first time in many days. Once his men had eaten their fill, Lee pressed on, crossing the Appomattox River and burning the bridges behind him. But even that failed to hold back Grant's forces, and Lee continued to feel the Union commander's presence just miles behind him. That evening, Lee received an invitation from Grant to surrender, an offer he quickly refused. A tiny ray of hope remained: If Lee could get his men to Appomattox Station, he could feed them from supply trains from Lynchville and then swing south to Danville.

On April 8, Grant's army forced Lee into another rear-guard action to protect his remaining wagons. As Lee's men fought for their very survival, Sheridan's cavalry and infantry under E. O. C. Ord quickly moved past Lee's southern flank and drove into Appomattox Station, where they captured Lee's supply trains and placed themselves across his line of march. That evening, Lee's army entered Appomattox Court House and saw the extent of Sheridan's force. The Confederates were greatly outnumbered by heavily armed Union cavalry and infantry, far too many for them to engage. An assault would have been sheer suicide, and all knew it. The end had finally come for Lee's Army of Northern Virginia.

It was an agonizing decision for Lee, who told Gordon he would rather "die a thousand deaths." But he had no choice. If he didn't surrender, thousands more would needlessly die.

Sign of the Changing Times   **The following day, April 9—Palm Sunday—Lee put on his very best dress uniform, including a red silk sash, a jeweled sword given to him by some women in England, red-stitched spurred boots, and long gray gloves, known as gauntlets. He planned to meet with Grant to discuss surrender terms and wanted to look his best if Grant took him prisoner.**

Sheridan was about to launch one final attack on Lee's army when a single man in gray rode out from the opposing ranks carrying a white flag of truce. He told Sheridan that Lee was waiting to meet with Grant at the nearby home of a man named Wilmer McLean. Sheridan was at first skeptical, but he quickly ordered a cease-fire, and for a long moment, the two armies simply stood there staring at each other. Grant then rode up to Sheridan and was told that Lee was expecting him at the house below. "Well then," Grant said, "let's go up."

Grant and Lee were an exercise in contrast when they shook hands in Wilmer McLean's parlor. Lee looked resplendent in his finest dress uniform, and Grant, who had been nursing a severe headache that morning and hadn't had time to clean up, rode up mud spattered and disheveled. Grant arrived alone and found Lee standing with two aides. He removed his gloves and extended his hand to the man he had pursued for so long. The two officers then sat down as six of Grant's generals entered the room and stood behind their commander.

They discussed better times for a few moments, then Lee, who was anxious to get on with the sad business at hand, said: "I suppose, General Grant, that the object of our present meeting is fully understood. I asked to see you to ascertain upon what terms you would receive the surrender of my army."

Realizing the gravity of the situation and the pain his adversary must have felt, Grant did no gloating that day. Though he had won, he was in no mood to celebrate. He told Lee that his officers and men would have to surrender, then be paroled and disqualified from taking up arms again until properly exchanged, and that all arms, ammunition, and supplies were to be delivered up as captured property.

After signing the declaration of surrender, Lee stood up and shook Grant's hand one more time. He bowed to the other men in the room, all of whom knew they were witnessing history in the making, and walked silently out the door. On the porch, Lee put his riding gloves on and gazed for a moment toward the hillside where his ragtag army awaited his return. He absently drove his right fist into his left hand three times, then mounted his beloved horse Traveller and rode away to deliver the difficult news to his men.

On April 14, General Robert Anderson raised the American flag over Fort Sumter—the same flag he had been forced to lower exactly four years earlier. Later that evening, Lincoln was killed at Ford's Theatre by John Wilkes Booth. Others would die in skirmishes over the next few weeks, but in many ways, Lincoln was the final casualty in a war that took so many.

92.
LEE'S FINAL
ORDER

ON APRIL 10, 1865, General Robert E. Lee issued his final order—one of farewell—to the soldiers of the Army of Northern Virginia. It read:

"After four years of arduous service marked by unsurpassed courage and fortitude, the Army of Northern Virginia has been compelled to yield to overwhelming numbers and resources. I need not tell the brave survivors of so many hard fought battles, who have remained steadfast to the last, that I have consented to this result from no distrust of them; but feeling that valor and devotion could accomplish nothing that could compensate for the loss that must have attended the continuance of the contest, I have determined to avoid the useless sacrifice of those whose past services have endeared them to their countrymen.

By the terms of the agreement, officers and men can return to their homes and remain there until exchanged. You will take with you the satisfaction that proceeds from the consciousness of duty faithfully performed; and I earnestly pray that a Merciful God will extend to you his blessing and protection.

With an unceasing admiration of your constancy and devotion to your Country, and grateful remembrance of your kind and generous consideration of myself, I bid you all an affectionate farewell."

R.E. Lee, Genl.

93.
THE LINGERING
WAR

LEE'S SURRENDER AT APPOMATTOX Court House on April 9, 1865, effectively brought the Civil War to an end. However, Lee's surrender was not the conclusion of hostilities; three other Confederate commanders continued to do battle with the Union for another two and a half months.

On the Homefront On May 12 and 13, Lieutenant General E. Kirby Smith, unaware of Lee's surrender, waged the last land battle of the war in west Texas.

Smith's force of 300 rebels won a surprising victory at Palmito Ranch over more than 800 Union soldiers under Theodore Barrett. Smith's men disbanded after hearing that Richmond had fallen, but Smith refused to give up the fight and went to Houston to rally more troops. His plan never saw fruition, however, because Lieutenant General Simon Buckner, acting in Smith's name, surrendered the Trans-Mississippi Department in New Orleans on May 25.

And then there was Stand Waitie, leader of the Cherokee Nation and commander of the largest Native American force in the Confederate Army. Waitie continued to wage war against the North until he was finally convinced to surrender to Lieutenant Colonel Asa C. Matthews on June 23, 1865.

94.
Arlington National Cemetery, a Final Resting Place

ONE OF CONFEDERATE GENERAL Robert E. Lee's greatest contributions to the United States—albeit unwittingly—was the land that currently serves as the nation's most famous military burial ground, Arlington National Cemetery.

Lee's family home, located just across the Potomac River from Washington, D.C., was seized by the Union army shortly after Lee resigned his commission to fight for the Confederacy. The mansion house was turned into headquarters for officers supervising the defense of Washington, D.C., and the fields were used as campgrounds for Union troops. Shortly after the Battle of Gettysburg in July 1863, the U.S. government officially confiscated the land because Lee had not shown up in person, as required by law, to pay a property tax of $92.02.

In the spring of 1864, Secretary of War Edwin Stanton instructed Quartermaster General Montgomery Meigs to find a suitable location for a new military cemetery. Meigs chose the Lee estate, which offered expansive land and a fitting view of the nation's capital. Meigs also enjoyed the irony of using the home of one of the Confederacy's most famous generals as a final resting place for the Union dead.

95.
THE PLOT AGAINST LINCOLN

THE ASSASSINATION OF ABRAHAM LINCOLN was not the act of a single disgruntled Confederate sympathizer—it was part of a wide-ranging conspiracy to avenge the South. Booth and several associates spent months planning to kidnap the president and exchange him for Confederate prisoners of war and possibly a peace treaty between the warring sides. However, as the Confederacy itself started to fall, Booth changed his plans and decided to kill Lincoln instead. Also on the conspirators' hit list were Vice President Johnson, Secretary of State Seward, and General Ulysses S. Grant. Lewis Powell was sent to assassinate Seward at his home, but he managed only to wound him, thanks in part to the heavy neck brace Seward was wearing at the time of the attack. Powell also wounded two of Seward's sons, a male nurse, and a state department messenger before fleeing.

After shooting Lincoln, Booth escaped by racing over the Navy Yard Bridge. He was met by an accomplice named David Herold, and the men stopped at the home of Dr. Samuel A. Mudd, who set Booth's broken leg. Booth and Herold then fled to the home of a fellow Confederate sympathizer, who hid them from authorities for almost a week. The two men then crossed the Rapahannock River, where they stopped at the farm of Richard Garrett. A couple of days later, Booth and Herold were surrounded by Union cavalry while sleeping in Garrett's tobacco barn. The soldiers ordered the assassin and his henchman to surrender. Herold immediately gave up, but Booth refused. The barn was set ablaze, and Booth was shot and killed. A soldier named Boston Corbett took credit for killing Booth, and while there have been claims that Booth might have committed suicide, it appears he was shot by Corbett.

On the Homefront **Not surprisingly, rumors of a large Confederate conspiracy in the death of Lincoln and the attacks on his cabinet swept through Washington. Some rumors suggested that Jefferson Davis and other prominent Confederate officials were in on the plot, but such was not the case; Booth and his cadre of Union haters had worked alone.**

In trials that were held before a Military Commission, all of the conspirators were found guilty, and four of them were executed by hanging. Three others, including Samuel Mudd, the doctor who set Booth's broken leg, were sentenced to life imprisonment, though Mudd served only four years before being pardoned and released. John Surratt, in whose boarding house the bizarre plot was conceived, managed to escape to Canada, then Europe, and finally the Papal States. He was arrested in 1866 and brought home for trial, but a hung jury freed him.

96.
THE CAPTURE OF
JEFFERSON DAVIS

BY THE END OF MARCH 1865, it became evident that despite the best efforts of Robert E. Lee and his dedicated but ragtag army, the Confederate capital of Richmond could not be held. On April 2, Lee warned Davis that he could no longer hold back the Union army and strongly suggested that Davis and his cabinet leave Richmond as soon as possible. Davis and others gathered what they could—including the Confederate treasury's remaining gold worth more than $500,000, Confederate bank notes, negotiable bonds, and a chest full of jewels—and boarded a train for Danville, Virginia. A day later, Union troops entered Richmond and Petersburg.

Davis had hoped to establish a new Confederate capital in Danville and continue the war against the North with Lee in charge, but it simply wasn't meant to be. Following Lee's surrender to Grant on April 9, Davis and his cabinet scattered to escape arrest. Davis continued south into Georgia, where he was reunited with his wife and family, and planned to travel to either Texas or Mexico, where he and many other members of the Confederacy hoped to find sanctuary. However, the federal army wasn't about to let Davis escape. They pursued him with dogged determination, especially after President Andrew Johnson (wrongly) named him a conspirator in the assassination of Abraham Lincoln.

Davis was finally captured near Irwinville, Georgia, on May 10 by a detachment of the Fourth Michigan Cavalry. He was taken with his wife and children to Macon, Georgia, and along the way was forced to endure the constant taunts of Union soldiers singing, "We'll hang Jeff Davis from a sour apple tree." On May 22, Davis was imprisoned in Fort Monroe, Virginia, and forced into shackles. Still proud and defiant, he resisted being chained and finally had to be subdued by his jailers. Davis sat in Fort Monroe for almost two years without benefit of trial, under constant watch by soldiers who had orders never to speak to him.

Davis suffered health problems during his incarceration. Already in frail health, captivity only exacerbated his weak physical condition. A light burned constantly in his dank cell, and he was not allowed even a moment of fresh air. It was as if officials in Washington wanted to make doubly sure that the defeated president of the Confederacy was thoroughly punished for his crimes. Ultimately, Dr. John Craven intervened on his behalf. The physician tended to Davis's health and made sure that his imprisonment was made more bearable by providing Davis with whatever comforts he could arrange.

The national press brought Davis's plight to the world and vocal demands for better treatment helped make Davis's imprisonment a little more tolerable. He was soon allowed to take walks on the prison grounds, and his health gradually improved. Davis was finally released on $100,000 bail. His surety bond was signed by newspaper publisher Horace Greeley and another vocal abolitionist named Gerrit Smith. A free man, Davis found himself with neither a home to return to nor a dollar in his wallet; the proud and defiant president of the Confederacy was now a pauper. All charges against Jefferson Davis were finally dropped by the federal government in 1869.

Davis lived another two decades. He traveled for a while, then settled in Mississippi, where he spent his time writing his memoir, *The Rise and Fall of the Confederate Government*. Davis never retracted a single word, thought, or deed and remained an unrepentant Confederate until his death on December 9, 1889.

97.
THE 13TH,
ABOLISHING,
AMENDMENT

THE THIRTEENTH AMENDMENT, RATIFIED at the end of 1865, officially abolished slavery. It read as follows:

> **Section 1**—Neither slavery nor involuntary servitude, except as punishment for crime whereof the party shall have been duly convicted, shall exist within the United States, or any place subject to their jurisdiction.

> **Section 2**—Congress shall have power to enforce this article by appropriate legislation.

Its ratification ended the institution of forced servitude forever and made permanent what Lincoln had attempted to accomplish with the Emancipation Proclamation.

However, had things gone differently, the Thirteenth Amendment would have continued slavery rather than abolished it. In 1861, an amendment to that effect was proposed in a desperate attempt to avoid civil war and keep the Union whole. It was supported by nearly half of the congressional Republicans and the vast majority of Democrats and had passed both the

House and the Senate by the required two-thirds majority. However, the war erupted before the amendment could be ratified by three-quarters of the states.

Sign of the Changing Times   Lincoln's Emancipation Proclamation officially made the abolition of slavery a goal of the war, but because it was a wartime edict, it freed only slaves from states in armed rebellion against the Union.

There was a chance that it wouldn't apply once the war was over, and many believed the Supreme Court might rule the proclamation unconstitutional.

In an attempt to end slavery in the United States once and for all, Lincoln laid the groundwork for a Constitutional amendment abolishing the institution in 1864. The Democratic Party opposed ratification of the amendment, even though Lincoln tried to sweeten the pot by promoting financial compensation from the federal government to all slaveholders. But despite objections from the Democrats, the Republican-dominated Senate quickly passed the proposed amendment in April by a vote of 38–6. However, the House, which had far more Democrats, failed to give it the necessary two-thirds support. Lincoln called for a second vote after his re-election suggested national backing for emancipation, and the amendment passed in January 1865 by a vote of 119–56. Lincoln signed the amendment in a symbolic gesture the very next day, and eight states ratified it within a week. The passage of the Thirteenth Amendment was celebrated with a 100-gun salute from artillery batteries on Capitol Hill. However, it took eight months for the rest of the states to follow suit. The amendment was officially ratified on December 18, 1865, eight months after Lincoln was assassinated.

98.
Reconstructing
the South

RECONSTRUCTION—THE PROCESS OF rebuilding the war-torn South—began shortly after the fall of the Confederacy and would continue for approximately 12 years. The many policies enacted during this period by the U.S. Congress and Presidents Andrew Johnson and Ulysses S. Grant were designed to bring the seceded states back into the Union and aid displaced individuals, especially freed slaves. But many of the policies were also punitive; radical Republicans within Congress wanted to make sure that the rebellious South was sufficiently penalized for putting the nation through four years of war, and to ensure that such a thing would never happen again.

Abraham Lincoln tentatively began the process of Reconstruction in 1863 with the announcement of a policy for the reconstruction of Southerners who denounced the Confederacy. Lincoln was eager to extend a compassionate hand to the South, despite the trials and tribulations it had wrought, and this policy was one of his first endeavors in that direction.

On December 8, 1863, Lincoln issued a proclamation in which he offered a full pardon and amnesty to any recanting Confederate who took an oath of allegiance to the United States and to all of its laws and proclamations regarding the institution of slavery. The only exemptions to this offer of amnesty were Confederate government officials and high-ranking military officers.

In addition, the proclamation provided for the formation of a state government that would be recognized by the president when the number of persons taking the oath of allegiance reached 10 percent of the number of voters in 1860. Congress retained the right to decide whether to seat the senators and representatives elected from such states.

However, many in Congress were fearful that Lincoln's early program, which was quite moderate in tone, would leave intact the political and economic framework that made slavery a driving force in the South.

On the Homefront   **Many Congressmen believed Reconstruction should be more of a revolution in which the South was dismantled and rebuilt with more Northern sensibilities.**

Only then could freed slaves enjoy all of the benefits of citizenship, including the right to vote and to walk the streets without fear of persecution.

The first response to Lincoln's plan came from radical Republicans in the form of the Wade-Davis Bill, which offered more stringent criteria for rejoining the Union. Lincoln killed the bill with a pocket veto (meaning he didn't sign or return the bill to Congress before it adjourned for the year). By the end of the war, Congress had passed the Thirteenth Amendment, which abolished slavery throughout the Union and gave Congress the power and authority to enforce abolition with the proper legislation. Shortly after the passage of the Thirteenth Amendment, Congress established the Freedman's Bureau, which was a federally funded agency designed to distribute food, clothing, and other provisions to impoverished freedmen and to oversee "all subjects" relating to their condition and treatment in the South.

99.
THE FREEDMAN'S BUREAU HELPS FORMER SLAVES ADAPT

THE BUREAU OF REFUGEES, Freedmen, and Abandoned Lands was established by Congress on March 1, 1865, in an attempt to aid the more than four million former slaves who lived in the South at the end of the Civil War. In existence for only one year and hobbled by allegations of corruption as well as a lack of funds and manpower, the bureau still managed to do much for the uneducated and poverty-stricken African Americans who suddenly found themselves without homes, jobs, or money.

Congress created the Freedman's Bureau and gave it just one year to do its job. Its primary goal was to distribute food, clothing, fuel, and medical care to impoverished former slaves, as well as oversee their well-being and treatment. General Oliver Otis Howard, a well-respected Civil War veteran, was chosen to head the Bureau's 900 agents.

One of the agency's most difficult tasks was creating a judicial system that was fair to both blacks and whites. Not surprisingly, most Southerners weren't particularly eager to treat freed slaves fairly, so the bureau first established its own judicial authority with local agents setting up temporary three-man courts to hear disputes.

The Freedman's Bureau also worked diligently to bring former slaves into a free labor economy. Plantations were still integral to the Southern economy, and the agency strived to bring African-Americans into the workforce with fair wages and the opportunity for advancement. One way in which that was accomplished was through the distribution of land that had been confiscated or abandoned during the war. The initial pledge was '40 acres and a mule" to every freed slave, but only about 2,000 South Carolina and 1,5000 Georgia freedmen actually received the land as promised.

Another important agency concern was health care. The agency tried to strengthen existing health care facilities such as hospitals, as well as establish a series of rural health clinics. During its operation, the bureau helped nearly 500,000 freed slaves to receive medical attention.

100.
BLACK CODES SLOW TRUE SOVEREIGNTY

BLACK CODES WERE SPECIAL laws passed by many Southern governments during the first year of Reconstruction to prevent former slaves from enjoying the benefits of their freedom. They restricted blacks' rights to buy, own, and sell property; make legally binding contracts; serve on juries; own weapons; and vote or run for political office. Black Codes also restricted African Americans from working in various professions, enforced apprenticeship prerequisites, required blacks to carry travel passes and proof of residence, and denied them their Constitutional right to free assembly.

Between 1866 and 1877, Congress tried to eliminate Black Codes by appointing Northern governors to head Southern states. However, after Reconstruction ended and politicians were replaced by Southerners, versions of Black Codes—known as Jim Crow laws after a popular minstrel song of the era—once again became commonplace.

101.
JOHNSON TAKES OVER: REJOINING THE UNION

PRESIDENT ANDREW JOHNSON TRIED to continue Lincoln's moderate Reconstruction policies following Lincoln's assassination in April 1865. In May of that year, he granted amnesty and pardon, including the restoration of all property rights except for slaves, on all former Confederates who took an oath of loyalty to the Union and accepted emancipation. Johnson also appointed provisional governors to lead the Southern states in drafting new constitutions that would allow them to rejoin the Union.

However, what Johnson did not do, other than emancipation, was provide for the millions of slaves who suddenly found themselves free men and women. Johnson believed that the Southern states should decide for themselves the future of freedmen, a shortsighted position that led to the institution of numerous Black Codes—states laws designed to keep African Americans out of politics and "in their place."

Many Southern whites felt extreme anger and frustration at the abolition of slavery and often expressed their hatred for blacks with violence. Between

Conflict of Interest Johnson tried to make the restoration of the Union as painless as possible by appointing men loyal to the Union to lead the readmitted states. However, radical Republicans took a different tack. They felt that since the seceded states had been defeated in the war, they no longer had any rights and should be treated as conquered territories. In their eyes, black suffrage and equal rights were the most important goals of Reconstruction, followed by the rebuilding of the ravaged South.

1865 and 1866, more than 5,000 African Americans were killed or severely beaten because of the color of their skin. So vehement was this racial hatred that the federal government quickly realized military control would be necessary to slowly bring Southern blacks into the national mainstream.

Johnson faced other problems as well. Many in Congress felt that Reconstruction should be the responsibility of the legislative branch of government and that Johnson had overstepped his authority as president in instituting certain Reconstruction policies. In order to maintain control, Congress enacted the Reconstruction Act of 1867, which dramatically affected Johnson's moderate plans for the rebuilding of the war-ravaged South. The 11 Confederate states were divided into five military districts under commanders who had the authority to use the army to protect the lives and property of all citizens—especially blacks. New state constitutions were required to include a promise to ratify the Fourteenth Amendment (which granted citizenship to newly freed slaves and directed the federal government to protect citizens from arbitrary state actions, including Black Codes), a loyalty oath swearing allegiance to the Union, and a ban that prohibited former Confederate leaders from holding political office.

Reconstruction policies enacted by Congress achieved quite a bit, including the first public, tax-supported school systems in most Southern states. There were also strong attempts to broaden and strengthen the Southern economy through aid to railroads and other industries. Most important of all, blacks were finally given a voice in local, state, and federal government.

However, things were far from perfect in the New South. The region's economy continued to be dominated by agriculture, despite attempts to lure industry (a situation that would continue into the twentieth century), and many Southerners did all they could to keep African Americans from assuming their rightful place in society. For example, many Southern states made it extremely difficult for blacks to vote by enacting deliberately prohibitive laws such as the poll tax. Most blacks also received far lower wages than white workers, which prevented them from buying land and otherwise becoming financially independent. Southern African Americans may have found themselves out of bondage, but they were far from free. It wasn't until the civil rights movement of the 1960s that many of their invisible shackles were finally removed.

Index

A

Abolition movement, 24–26. *See also* Slavery
  American Anti-Slavery Society and, 24–25
  Bleeding Kansas and, 27–28
  Dred Scott ruling and, 23
  Frederick Douglass and, 20–21, 25
  Fugitive Slave Act and, 14–15, 25
  John Brown and, 18–20, 28
  many voices of, 24–26
  Salmon P. Chase and, 43
  in the South, 26
  13th Amendment and, 225–27, 229
  William Lloyd Garrison and, 17–18, 21, 24
African American soldiers, 169–72
American Anti-Slavery Society, 24–25
Amputations, 151, 164
Anderson, Robert, 85, 86–87, 216
Andersonville, 161–63
Antietam, 94–96, 158
Appomattox Court House, 214–16
Arlington National Cemetery, 219–20

Artillery, 140–41
Atlanta, burning of, 112–15

B

Barton, Clara, 163, 165–66
Battles. *See also* Horrors of war; Naval battles
  Antietam, 94–96, 158
  Atlanta, 112–15
  Bull Run (First Battle), 64, 65, 87–90
  Bull Run (Second Battle), 72, 74, 97, 166
  Chancellorsville, 96–98
  Chattanooga, 104–6
  Chickamauga, 101–3
  final, 207–9
  Fort Sumter, 31, 32, 85–87
  Gettysburg, 99–100, 151–52
  Nashville, 115–17
  Petersburg, 117–20, 205, 207–8, 209
  Shiloh, 68, 91–93, 183
  Spotsylvania, 110–12
  Wilderness, 107–9

Beauregard, Pierre G. T, 41, 76, 86, 88–89, 91, 92–93, 118, 125
Beginning of Civil War, 87
Benjamin, Judah P., 44–45, 137
Bible, slavery and, 200–201
Black Codes after, 231, 232–34
Bleeding Kansas, 27–28
Blockade of Southern ports, 47, 54, 58, 120–21, 127, 130, 206
Booth, John Wilkes, 216, 220, 221
Boyd, Belle, 179–80
Brady, Matthew, 177–78
Bragg, Braxton, 76, 101–2, 103, 104, 105, 106
Brown, John, 18–20, 28
Buchanan, James, 29–30
Bull Run (First Battle), 64, 65, 87–90
Bull Run (Second Battle), 72, 74, 97, 166
Bureau of Refugees, Freedmen, and Abandoned Lands, 229–30
Burleigh, Charles Calistus, 26
Burnside, Ambrose, 73, 96, 97, 105
Butler, Benjamin Franklin, 64–65, 88, 123, 166

C
Calhoun, John C., 15–16

Camp life, 154–56
Cannons, 140–41
Casualty statistics, 157–59
Causes of Civil War. *See also* Abolition movement; Slavery demographics and economics, 2–4 states' rights, 6–7
Chancellorsville, 96–98
Chaos, on battlefield, 156–57
Chase, Salmon P., 43, 83
Chattanooga, Battle of, 104–6
Chickamauga, 101–3
Children, in line of fire, 182–83
City life, during war, 194–96
Clem, Johnny, 183
Clothing and uniforms, 144–46
Compromise of 1850, 6–7
Confederacy
  border states, 38–39
  cabinet members, 44–45
  as underdog, 37
Confederate Army. *See also* Lee, Robert E.
  amateur soldiers of, 79–80
  battles. *See* Battles; Naval battles
  call to arms, 79
  commanders, 74–75
  formation of, 41
  Lincoln relatives in, 193

Conspiracy, against Lincoln and others, 220–22
Custer, George, 75

D

Davis, Jefferson
    Alexander Hamilton Stephens and, 57–58
    capture of, 222–24
    Confederate officers and, 41, 100
    end of war and, 73, 204, 205, 209, 210–12
    political life/Southern leader, 52–55
Davis, Varina Howell, 52, 62–64
Death statistics, 157–59
Death toll, xii
Democratic Party
    on abolition amendment, 226
    Jefferson Davis and, 53, 62
    split into two factions, 35–36
Dix, Dorothea, 166–67
Doctrine of nullification, 15–16
Douglas, Stephen, 50–52
    debates with Lincoln, 48–50
    Kansas-Nebraska Act of, 27, 34, 50–51
    working to save Union, 30–31
Douglass, Frederick, 20–21, 25

Dred Scott ruling, 22–23

E

Economics
    funding war and, 83–84
    growth of America and, 188–90
    impacting pre-war tensions, 3–4
    at time of secession, 33–34
Effects of Civil War
    on all Americans, 186–87
    changing family roles, 190–92
    on city life, 194–96
    dividing families, 193–94
    on farm life, 196–98
    growth of America and, 188–90
    overview, 185–86
    on plantation life, 198–99
Ellet, Charles, 125–26
Emancipation Proclamation, 36, 56, 94, 171, 225, 226
End of Civil War
    final battles, 207–9
    Hampton Roads peace conference, 210–11
    imminence of, 204–6, 211–14
    Jefferson Davis and, 73, 204, 205, 209, 210–12, 222–24
    Lee's final order, 216–17
    Lee surrendering, 69, 73, 211–16

lingering hostilities after, 217–18

overview, 203

England, position on War, 46–48, 206

Espionage, 179–80

Ethnicity of soldiers, 173–74. *See also* African American soldiers

Europe, choosing sides, 45–48

Expansionism, Manifest Destiny and, 4–7

F

Families

roles within, war changing, 190–92

war dividing, 193–94

Farm life, war affecting, 196–98

Farragut, David, 123–24, 127–28

Flags, 149–50

Forrest, Nathan Bedford, 92, 103, 117

Fort Sumter

fall of, 31, 32, 85–87

left vulnerable, 30, 85–86

Union return to, 216

Freedman's Bureau, 229–30

Fugitive Slave Act, 14–15, 25

Funding war, 83–84

G

Garrison, William Lloyd, 17–18, 21, 24

Gettysburg, 99–100, 151–52

Gordon, John, 109, 119, 208, 213

Grant, Ulysses S.

at Appomattox Court House, 214–16

biographical sketch, 66–67

at Chattanooga, 104–6

final battles, 207–9

final years, 69

first military action, 67–68

Lee surrendering to, 69, 73, 211–16

at Petersburg, 117–20

as president, 69

promoted to general, 68

at Shiloh, 91–93

at Spotsylvania, 110–12

war record, 68–69

at Wilderness, 107–9

Growth of America, 188–90

Guns. *See* Weapons

H

Halleck, Henry, 93, 125

Hamlin, Hannibal, 55–56

Hampton Roads peace conference, 210–11

Hancock, Winfield Scott, 99, 110–11

Herold, David, 221

Hill, Daniel, 95, 105

Hood, John B., 113–17

Hooker, Joseph, 75, 95, 96–98, 106

Horrors of war
African American soldiers and, 169–72
amputations, 151, 164
Andersonville POW camp, 161–63
battlefield chaos, 156–57
camp life, 154–56
casualty statistics, 157–59
chronicling, 175–78
Clara Barton and, 165–66
Dorothea Dix and, 166–67
espionage and, 179–80
medical care, 163–64, 167–68
photographs of, 177–78
prisoners and exchanges, 159–61
women/children in line of fire, 181–83

Housing, 189–90

I

Internal Revenue Act, 83–84

Ironclad ships, 82, 122, 194

characteristics/innovations of, 142–44
at Memphis, 125–26
at Mobile Bay, 127–28
Monitor vs. *Merrimack*, 129–30

J

Jackson, Thomas "Stonewall," 72, 73, 89, 94, 95, 97–98

Jim Crow laws (Black Codes), 231, 232–34

Johnson, Andrew, 55, 56, 63, 220, 223, 232–34

Johnston, Albert Sidney, 41, 75–76, 91–93

Johnston, Joseph E., 41, 69, 72, 88–90, 113, 119, 208

Journalists, covering war, 175–78

K

Kansas, violence in, 27–28

Kansas–Nebraska Act, 27, 34, 50–51

L

Lee, Robert E., 41
at Appomattox Court House, 214–16
biographical sketch, 70–71
conflicted allegiance of, 70
final battles, 207–9

final order of, 216–17
greatest victory, 96–98
home of, as Arlington National
    Cemetery, 219–20
offered Union command, 70
offering resignation, 100
at Petersburg, 117–20
postwar life, 74
at Spotsylvania, 110–12
surrendering to Grant, 69, 73,
    211–16
war record, 71–74
at Wilderness, 107–9
Lincoln, Abraham
assassination of, 216, 220–22
on black soldiers, 170
debates with Douglas, 48–50
demands for end of war, 211
election of, secession and, 29, 30
ending slavery, 226–27
plot against, 220–22
reconstruction policy, 227–29
relatives in Confederate Army, 193
wife and children, 59–61
Lincoln, Mary Todd, 59–61
Longstreet, James, 94, 101, 102–3,
    105, 108–9

M
Manifest Destiny, 4–7
Mason-Dixon line, 32–33
McClellan, George B, 41, 72, 94–
    95, 96
McDowell, Irvin, 72, 88–89
Meade, George G., 68, 74–75, 100,
    109
Medical care, 163–64, 167–68
Memphis, 125–26
Mexican War, 4–5, 53, 67, 71, 78,
    80
Missouri Compromise, 5–7
Mobile Bay, 127–28
Monitor vs. *Merrimack*, 129–30
Mudd, Samuel, 221
Music, on battlefield, 151–52

N
Nashville, Battle of, 115–17
Naval battles, 120–30. *See also*
    Ironclad ships
blockade of Southern ports, 47, 54,
    58, 120–21, 127, 130, 206
condition of navies and, 121–22
families as enemies in, 194
Memphis, 125–26
Mobile Bay, 127–28
Monitor vs. *Merrimack*, 129–30

101 THINGS YOU DIDN'T KNOW ABOUT THE CIVIL WAR

New Orleans, 122–24
  ram ships and, 125–26
New Orleans, Battle of, 122–24
Newspaper coverage, 175–76
Northern Army. *See* Union Army

P

Parker, Theodore, 25
Petersburg, 117–20, 205, 207–8, 209
Photography, of war, 177–78
Pickett, George, 99–100, 119, 208–9
Plantation life, war affecting, 198–99
Polk, Leonidas, 102, 103, 105
Porter, David, 123
Prisoners of war, 159–63

R

Ram ships, 125–26
Reconstruction, 210–11, 227–29, 233–34
Regiment, 54th Massachusetts, 171–72
Republican Party
  Abraham Lincoln and, 23, 29
  emancipation view of, 35–36
  origin of, 34–35

radical faction opposing Reconstruction, 227, 228, 233
Salmon P. Chase and, 43
Stephen Douglas and, 50
Richmond, fall of, 119–20, 204, 207, 209, 222
Rosecrans, William, 101–2, 104

S

Scott, Dred, 22–23
Scott, Winfield, 41
Secession, 29–32, 33
Sedgwick, John, 98
Seward, William Henry, 42–43, 58–59, 86, 210, 211, 220
Sheridan, Philip, 204, 208–9, 212, 213–15
Sherman, William T.
  at Chattanooga, 105–6
  contributing to victory, 204, 205
  march to the sea, 37, 69, 112, 198
  on the press, 177
  at Shiloh, 92
  taking Atlanta, 112–15
Shiloh, 68, 91–93, 183
Ships. *See* Ironclad ships; Naval battles
Slavery, xi–xii. *See also* Abolition movement

African slave trade, 10–11
background and growth of, 8–9
Bible and, 200–201
Black Codes after, 231, 232–34
as cause of war, 2, 8–9
Compromise of 1850 and, 6–7
doctrine of nullification and,
    15–16
end of, 225–27, 229
Freedman's Bureau helping freed
    slaves, 229–30
Fugitive Slave Act, 13–14
harrowing trips across ocean,
    10–11
Missouri Compromise and, 5–7
Nat Turner story, 12–13
plantation life and, 198–99
Western expansion inflaming
    issue, 5–7
Spies, 179–80
Spotsylvania, 110–12
States' rights, 6–7
Stephens, Alexander Hamilton, 57–
    59, 211
Stuart, Jeb, 19–20, 75, 97, 98, 99,
    100
Surratt, John, 221–22
Surrender, of Lee to Grant, 69, 73,
    211–16
Swords and sabers, 138–39

T
Taxes, 83–84
Thirteenth Amendment, 225–27,
    229
Thomas, George Henry, 102–3,
    104, 106, 116
Toombs, Robert, 44
Truth, Sojourner (Isabella
    Baumfree), 26
Tubman, Harriet, 26
Turner, Nat, 12–13

U
Uniforms and clothing, 144–48
Union
    border states, 38–39
    cabinet members, 42–43
    incompetent leadership, 64–65
    secession of Southern states, 29–
        32, 33
Union Army. *See also* Grant,
    Ulysses S.
    amateur soldiers of, 78–80
    battles. *See* Battles; Naval battles
    call to arms, 40–41, 78–79
    commanders, 74–75

W
Warfare, changes in, 81–82

Weapons. *See also* Ironclad ships
    artillery, 140–41
    changes in, overview, 81–82
    handguns, 136–37
    muskets and rifles, 134–35
    overview, 131–32
    small arms, overview, 132–33
    swords and sabers, 138–39
Wilderness, Battle of, 107–9
Wirz, Henry, 162–63
Women
    in line of fire, 181–82
    new roles for, xi, 191–92

About the Author

Thomas R. Turner, Ph.D., is a professor of History at Bridgewater State College, Bridgewater, MA, where he has taught since 1971. Dr. Turner's academic specialty is the assassination of Abraham Lincoln. He has published two books on the topic, *Beware the People Weeping* and *The Assassination of Abraham Lincoln*. He is the editor of the *Lincoln Herald*, past president of the Lincoln Group of Boston, a member of the advisory board of the Lincoln Forum, and a member of the Lincoln Prize Committee at Gettysburg College.